Psychology
as a Major

San Diego Christian College
2100 Greenfield Drive
El Cajon, CA 92019

Psychology
as a Major

Is It Right for Me and
What Can I Do With
My Degree?

DONNA E. PALLADINO SCHULTHEISS

American Psychological Association
Washington, DC

Published by
American Psychological Association
750 First Street, NE
Washington, DC 20002
www.apa.org

To order
APA Order Department
P.O. Box 92984
Washington, DC 20090-2984
Tel: (800) 374-2721; Direct: (202) 336-5510
Fax: (202) 336-5502; TDD/TTY: (202) 336-6123
Online: www.apa.org/books/
E-mail: order@apa.org

In the U.K., Europe, Africa, and the Middle East, copies may be ordered from
American Psychological Association
3 Henrietta Street
Covent Garden, London
WC2E 8LU England

Typeset in Meridien by Stephen McDougal, Mechanicsville, MD

Printer: McNaughton & Gunn, Inc., Saline, MI
Cover Designer: Naylor Design, Washington, DC
Technical/Production Editor: Harriet Kaplan

The opinions and statements published are the responsibility of the authors, and such opinions and statements do not necessarily represent the policies of the American Psychological Association.

Library of Congress Cataloging-in-Publication Data

Schultheiss, Donna E. Palladino
  Psychology as a major : is it right for me and what can I do with my degree? /
Donna E. Palladino Schultheiss. — 1st ed.
    p. cm.
  Includes bibliographical references and index.
  ISBN-13: 978-1-4338-0336-9
  ISBN-10: 1-4338-0336-4
  1. Psychology—Study and teaching (Higher) 2. Psychology—Vocational guidance. I. Title.

  BF77.P35 2008
  150.71′1—dc22   2007047613

British Library Cataloguing-in-Publication Data
A CIP record is available from the British Library.

Printed in the United States of America
First Edition

In memory of my husband,
Curt,
and to our three wonderful sons,
Matthew,
Joshua,
and Andrew

Contents

List of Exhibits and Tables

Exhibits

Tables

Acknowledgments

Many people have contributed in countless ways to this book. I thank Lansing Hays, acquisitions editor for the American Psychological Association Books Department, for his inspiration and enthusiasm for the book. His insightful input helped to shape its content and focus. I thank Linda McCarter, who succeeded Lansing as acquisitions editor. Our paths crossed in brief yet significant ways. Ron Teeter has been a stellar resource as the development editor who brought this book through to the production phase. His careful editing and keen insight helped to make this book much better than it would have been without his input. Many thanks go to Harriet Kaplan, production editor, whose meticulous attention to detail was invaluable. I offer sincere thanks to Jessica Kohout, who provided a thoughtful review and made valuable contributions of survey data. I also thank the other anonymous reviewers whose comments were essential in helping to improve this book. Special thanks go to Briana Keller, who was among the first to read and review many chapters of this book; to Robert Clapp and his students for their helpful comments; and to my graduate assistant Mary Clare Smith, who made a meaningful contribution by introducing me to mindfulness practices.

Itamar Gati, professor at Hebrew University of Jerusalem, Israel, a world-renowned scholar in career decision making, and his graduate student, Shiri Tal, are due countless thanks for their invaluable review and comments on the decision-making chapters. I feel privileged to share their work with the readers of this book. I am indebted to several other colleagues for their permission to include their assessment instruments in this book: David Blustein, Michael Ellis, Luanna Devenis, Linda Subich, Richard Lenox, and Graham Stead.

Many vocational psychologists have dedicated their careers to assisting people with career exploration, planning, and decision making. Their scholarly contributions laid the groundwork for this book.

A special thanks goes to my parents, Al and Chris Palladino, for their support in my early decision to make psychology my future. Finally, many thanks go to my family. Thanks, boys, for your patience with the many hours I spent writing. My deepest heartfelt thanks goes to my late husband, Curt, who supported and nurtured me throughout the writing of this book. I thank him for his unwavering belief in me, enduring love and encouragement, and humor when I needed it most. His love and spirit will live on in me forever.

Psychology
as a Major

Introduction

P sychology concerns all aspects of human experience. Maybe that is why about 82,000 students (National Center on Educational Statistics, n.d.) earn a bachelor's degree in psychology each year! Yes, each year. And, that number does not include all of the students who choose psychology as a minor or simply find psychology fascinating. Psychology is a helping profession with rich opportunities to make a difference in people's lives across the lifespan, from infancy to the elderly. Many exciting areas of research help us better understand why people behave, think, and feel the way they do. Psychology continues to expand its boundaries as contemporary trends keep pace with technological advances and global changes. For example, cutting-edge technology has introduced fascinating new imaging techniques for brain research. Globalization has stimulated enriching multicultural experiences and interactions with diverse groups of people across the globe. If you are curious about human behavior, thought, and emotion, you will be pleased to learn all that psychology has to offer.

Because you have opened a book entitled *Psychology as a Major: Is It Right for Me and What Can I Do With My Degree?* you are probably wondering just that. Whether you are considering psychology as an undergraduate major, have already declared psychology as a major, or are simply curious as to what psychology is about, this book will help you evaluate whether psychology is the right choice for you. The individual chapters will help you understand psychology as a science and a profession and what a major in psychology entails. It will give you a road map for succeeding in the major and describe the kinds of jobs possible with a bachelor's, master's, or doctorate in psychology. You will have a chance to acquaint yourself, and even work with, the tools of the trade by completing various self-assessments.

In reading this book you will also learn more about yourself! That's right. Making educational and career decisions involves not only learning more about occupations, it also means learning more about yourself and your own unique interests, skills, abilities, and values. To this end, this book draws on the career counseling literature to aid you in what will be an extensive journey of self-exploration, with step-by-step guides to decision making and strategies for managing the inevitable stresses associated with making important life decisions. It integrates tried-and-true strategies that emphasize the importance of self-exploration and occupational exploration in the career decision-making process. The tools presented in this book include self-assessments and other powerful tools to enhance self-understanding and increase your self-knowledge. Creative strategies to seek out essential information about the world of work in psychology are also provided. Finally, each chapter suggests Web sites and readings for further information on various topics.

Making life decisions can be challenging and anxiety producing. You may be like many people who hold a number of myths and fears about making important decisions like choosing a college major. Decision making is a skill, and you will find in these pages the information and tools you need to make intelligent, informed, and thoughtful decisions. Skills and strategies for success can be learned, and that is what this book is all about: learning the essential strategies you need to make good decisions and manage the anxiety that often accompanies the stress of choosing a college major. You will leave these pages with the confidence and knowledge you need to make successful important decisions about your future. There is so much to learn about psychology. Let's get started!

The book is organized to first provide information about psychology and then discuss strategies to succeed as a psychology major.

- Chapter 1 offers an introduction to what psychology is all about, including the science of psychology, the tasks and problems taken on by psychologists, and the variety of settings in which psychologists work. Subfields of the discipline are described along with the similarities and differences between psychology and other helping professions.
- Chapter 2 describes what you can expect as an undergraduate psychology major. It includes a discussion of courses and topics of study and why a major in psychology is a good choice for the de-

velopment of skills and abilities that can be transferred to a wide variety of settings.

The next several chapters of the book focus on strategies to help you to decide whether psychology is the right major for you.

- Chapter 3 offers tools, including self-assessments and experiential exercises, for exploring whether your interests, abilities, values, and preferences match the requirements and attributes of the tasks and environments of various psychology-related work settings.

- Chapter 4 provides ideas about where to turn if you are still having difficulty deciding on a college major. The chapter discusses career counseling, including how to access these services, and other important aspects of career planning.

- Chapter 5 offers tips for managing the stress that sometimes occurs as you work through the process of choosing a major.

- Chapter 6 offers information to help you get the most out of your major in psychology. The importance of finding a mentor, engaging in research, seeking out field experiences in the community, and becoming involved in psychology clubs and professional organizations is emphasized.

- The emphasis of chapter 7 is twofold. First, there is a discussion of the strength in multicultural diversity among psychology professionals. This includes a discussion of the need for people from diverse backgrounds to enter the field and the special opportunities that await you. Second, this chapter presents the challenges and opportunities that arise from living and working in a multiculturally diverse world. Understanding and appreciating cultural diversity as well as the path toward multicultural competence are explored.

Interested in working after college or in graduate study in psychology or another field? The final two chapters of the book focus on the possibilities that await you after you earn a bachelor's degree in psychology.

- Chapter 8 conveys the breadth of occupational opportunities available to graduates with a bachelor's degree in psychology. This chapter also explores alternative career paths that require further graduate or professional school training in areas outside of psychology, including business and law.

- Chapter 9 will help you decide whether a graduate degree in psychology is a desirable goal for you. This final chapter covers graduate training and the skills and abilities required of a psychologist.

I hope that you find the information contained in these pages useful as you progress through your own decision-making process and plan your future. More important, I hope this book will increase your curiosity and get you excited and motivated about the possibilities of a major, and a career, in psychology. Enjoy your journey!

What Is Psychology? | 1

P sychology is the scientific study of behavior and mental processes, such as thoughts, emotions, perception, and intelligence. As you will soon learn, psychology is a discipline that spans many content areas and work settings. Although most people probably think of psychologists as people who conduct psychotherapy in a clinic or private office, the field of psychology is much broader. In addition to diagnosing and treating people with emotional and mental disorders, psychologists are concerned with a diverse range of content areas such as how the brain functions and how it relates to behavior and emotion; the interface of psychology and the law; and helping athletes improve their performance through setting goals, improving motivation, and managing anxiety. Other tasks and problems taken on by psychologists include assessing intelligence, personality, and other personal characteristics; enhancing social relationships; facilitating healthy development; improving wellness; promoting social justice; and teaching future psychologists and others interested in human functioning.

Many psychologists conduct basic and applied research to learn more about behavior across diverse social and cultural contexts. They do this by applying the scientific methods of observation, data collection, data analysis, and interpretation to carefully test hypotheses. Like many scientific disciplines, psychology integrates *research* (the study of human and animal behaviors to promote knowledge and facilitate practice) and *practice* (the application of research to solve problems and promote healthy functioning and development). This means that the knowledge gained through research contributes to and influences practice and that practice contributes to and stimulates questions to be addressed through psychological research.

Earning a bachelor's degree in psychology can provide you with a number of career path options. The skills you will learn as a psychology major (e.g., effective communication, problem solving, teamwork) will prepare you to be an ideal candidate for many jobs. People with undergraduate degrees in psychology are well suited for jobs involving helping others, so the human services field attracts many graduates. Others find that they are qualified for and interested in a number of diverse occupations, including those in business, law, health care, and education, to name a few.

Although the benefits of a bachelor's degree are rich, a doctorate is generally considered to be the entry-level degree for the independent, licensed practice of psychology as a profession. Earning a doctoral degree typically includes 5 years of study beyond the undergraduate years. The first 3 years of graduate training focuses primarily on required coursework. Most graduate students can expect to enroll in three to four courses per semester during this time. Unlike the coursework you take while you are an undergraduate, graduate study focuses specifically on your chosen content area. Therefore, all or most of your courses will be psychology courses, and few, if any, general education courses in other departments (such as history, literature, or language arts) will be required. During the 4th and 5th years of doctoral study, students are typically required to write a dissertation. A dissertation is usually based on an original scientific study that you plan and carry out under the supervision of an advisor. It requires intensive study of a particular topic of interest to you and of relevance to the field. Doctoral psychology programs that lead to eligibility for licensure as a psychologist (i.e., clinical, counseling, school, and industrial/organizational) also include supervised clinical training in university and community settings. In these programs, the final year of study consists of a full-time supervised internship in which you perform various clinical tasks, including diagnosing and treating emotional and mental disorders.

Licensure requirements for psychologists vary by state. The Association of State and Provincial Psychology Boards maintains a Web site (http:// www.asppb.org) with links to state psychology boards for information about licensure in each particular state.

Subfields of Psychology and Work Settings

There are a number of subfields within psychology and a variety of settings in which psychologists work. Many psychologists are service providers in clinics, hospitals, schools and universities, private practices, nonprofit organizations, and other settings. Others are professors, researchers, or administrators in universities, hospitals, businesses, and government agencies. Salaries of psychologists vary by the type of position, with applied psychologists (i.e., clinical, counseling, school, and industrial/organizational) earning on average $75,500 per year, more than assistant professors (from $49,171 in U.S. master's departments of psychology to $60,531 in U.S. doctoral departments of psychology) in their first 3 years of work after completing the doctoral degree. For more information on the salaries of doctoral-level psychologists, refer to chapter 9, this volume. You can get up-to-date salary information for psychology faculty on the Web site of the American Psychological Association Center for Psychology Workforce Analysis and Research (http://research.apa.org/). The most common subfields of psychology are discussed next.

CLINICAL PSYCHOLOGY

Clinical psychology is concerned with assessing and treating mental, emotional, and behavioral disorders. Problems that clinical psychologists treat range in severity from short-term crises, like a relationship breakup, to more severe and chronic mental illnesses, such as schizophrenia. Some clinical psychologists consult with physicians on physical problems that have underlying psychological causes and vice versa. Although many clinical psychologists have a general practice in which they treat a range of client problems, some psychologists specialize in treating specific disorders (such as phobias or depression) or specific age groups (such as children or the elderly). Clinical psychologists engage in psychotherapeutic practice, conduct research, teach in colleges and universities, and take on administrative positions in a variety of settings.

COGNITIVE AND PERCEPTUAL PSYCHOLOGY

Cognitive and perceptual psychologists study attention, thinking, reasoning, memory, judgment, decision making, problem solving, and visual and auditory perception. They are interested in whether the thoughts of people with problems such as depression have biological bases. They study how people learn and the ways in which they apply what they have learned. Other interests of cognitive and perceptual psychologists include how language is produced, analyzed, and understood. Cognitive and perceptual psychologists typically work in college, university, or research facilities.

COUNSELING PSYCHOLOGY

Counseling psychology focuses on improving people's personal and interpersonal functioning across the life span. This subfield is unique in that it focuses on the spectrum of wellness and mental health from normal developmental concerns and transitions to more serious emotional and mental disorders. Counseling psychologists help people recognize and develop their strengths and resources to cope with life transitions and difficulties. They conduct research, apply interventions, and evaluate services. In addition to working with individuals, counseling psychologists work with groups and organizations to advance personal and group development and to address organizational concerns. Work settings include academia, counseling centers, independent practice, hospitals, community mental health centers, business and industry, and schools.

DEVELOPMENTAL PSYCHOLOGY

Developmental psychology involves the study of psychological development during a person's life. Many developmental psychologists work with children and adolescents to ensure that they are meeting developmental milestones. For example, some work in day care centers, hospitals, child development centers, and educational institutions. The work of developmental psychologists in these settings includes assessment and intervention, as well as consultation on program development, implementation, and evaluation. An increasing number work with older adults in long-term care facilities. Others teach in colleges and universities and conduct research. Research conducted by developmental psychologists focuses on the emotional, intellectual, moral, social, and physical development of children, adolescents, and adults.

EDUCATIONAL PSYCHOLOGY

Educational psychologists are concerned with the process of effective teaching and learning. They conduct research as well as develop, implement, and evaluate methods to improve the effectiveness of educational programs and curricula. Educational psychologists are interested in factors associated with learning processes (including academic ability, self-efficacy, motivation, and learning styles), instructional methods (curricula and instruction, teacher characteristics), and academic environments (including academic climate). Some educational psychologists teach and conduct research in colleges and universities in both psychology departments and schools of education.

EXPERIMENTAL PSYCHOLOGY

Experimental psychologists study the basic processes involved in storing, retrieving, expressing, and applying knowledge. They are interested in a variety of psychological phenomena, including cognitive processes, sensation, perception, language, communication, learning, and conditioning. They also are interested in comparative psychology, the study of the behavior of animals other than human beings. Experimental psychologists use empirical methods to study both humans and nonhumans. Most experimental psychologists work in academic settings teaching and conducting research. Others are employed by research institutions, business, industry, and government.

FORENSIC PSYCHOLOGY

Forensic psychology, the application of psychology to the criminal justice system, represents the intersection of psychology and law. It applies psychological principles to legal issues such as child custody, juror selection, eyewitness testimony, and competence to stand trial. Forensic psychologists often work in the courts, prisons, or special agencies concerned with forensic assessment and the treatment of mentally ill offenders. Some forensic psychologists work on a variety of civil matters, including lawsuits and insurance claims where emotional suffering is a part of the claim. Others make determinations such as whether or not an aged or ill person is competent to make decisions or whether a death was an accident or suicide. Some forensic psychologists are involved in public policy and in the design of correctional facilities and prisons.

HEALTH PSYCHOLOGY

Health psychologists focus on how biological and psychological factors affect health and the course and outcome of illness. They also focus on social factors that affect the experience of illness. More specifically, health psychologists study how people respond to medical illness and treatment (including coping skills and medical compliance), pain management, and healthy and unhealthy lifestyles (including diet and the use of alcohol, drugs, and tobacco). Health psychologists often work in teams with physicians and other medical personnel. They also study the causes and the prevention and treatment of national health problems, including HIV/AIDS, teenage pregnancy, smoking, substance abuse, and physical inactivity. Health psychologists work in applied settings such as hospitals and clinics but also are employed in academic and research settings such as universities.

INDUSTRIAL/ORGANIZATIONAL PSYCHOLOGY

Industrial/organizational (I/O) psychology includes the study of behavior in organizational and work settings. It is particularly focused on the application of the methods, knowledge, and principles of psychology to individuals and groups. I/O psychologists are interested in improving workplace productivity and the quality of work life. They are interested in the interdependence of individuals, organizations, and society as well as in the impact of government influences, growing consumer awareness, skill shortages, and the changing nature of work and the workforce. Issues that affect workplace behavior such as job satisfaction, motivation, organizational development, quality of work life, work and family integration, and consumer behavior are of primary concern. Some I/O psychologists are involved in the selection, training, and evaluation of employees. Many I/O psychologists work as applied psychologists or consultants to business and industry in the areas of strategic planning, organizational development, quality improvement, and implementing organizational change. Others work as researchers and teachers in university settings.

NEUROPSYCHOLOGY

Neuropsychologists focus on how behavior, emotion, and skills are related to brain structures and functioning. They often work with individuals following a stroke or other traumatic brain injury or with individuals who have dementia. Clinical neuropsychologists perform assessments to identify the extent of brain damage and the severity of impairment. In addition, they develop interventions to help people adapt or regain functioning to maximize their potential for independent living and quality of life. Researchers study topics such as how the brain stores and retrieves memories and how various diseases and injuries of the brain affect emotion, perception, and behavior. They often work with physicians who use advanced technology such as positron emission tomography (PET), single photon emission computed tomography, and functional magnetic resonance imaging (fMRI) to assess brain functioning. Neuropsychologists teach and conduct research in academic and medical settings and practice in hospitals, clinics, and independent practice.

QUANTITATIVE AND MEASUREMENT PSYCHOLOGY

Quantitative psychologists study and design new methods and techniques for collecting and analyzing research data. They often play specific and integral roles on research teams. Measurement psychologists are primarily concerned with *psychometrics* (creating psychological and other tests and assessing how well they actually measure what they are supposed to measure). Both quantitative and measurement psychologists are well trained in research methods, statistics, and computer applications. They typically work in research and academic settings.

REHABILITATION PSYCHOLOGY

Rehabilitation psychology applies psychological knowledge to the understanding of individuals with disabilities. Rehabilitation psychologists assist people with coping and adjusting to chronic, traumatic, or congenital injuries or illnesses that result in an array of physical, sensory, neurocognitive, emotional, and/or developmental disabilities. They help individuals reach their highest level of physical, psychological, and interpersonal functioning. To accomplish this, rehabilitation psychologists work with people to address personal factors (such as mood, self-esteem, and self-determination) that may interfere with their ability to do things. In addition to working directly with individuals and their families, rehabilitation psychologists serve as consultants on disability and health issues to attorneys, courts, government agencies, educational institutions, corporations, and insurance companies. They also are involved in research, teaching, public education, administration, program development, and the development of social policy and advocacy. They are employed by acute care hospitals and medical centers, rehabilitation centers, long-term care facilities, community agencies with disability services, and colleges and universities.

SCHOOL PSYCHOLOGY

School psychologists assess students' developmental needs, provide interventions, and coordinate educational, psychological, and behavioral health services. They also develop effective home and school partnerships to better help families and schools to meet the needs of children. School psychologists typically work individually with students and consult with teachers, principals, and parents regarding students' needs. Although school psychologists work primarily in schools, they also work in school-based health centers, social service agencies, and correctional facilities. School psychologists apply principles of learning to the development of competence within and outside schools. One of their main goals is to promote positive learning environments.

SOCIAL PSYCHOLOGY

Social psychologists study how a person's thoughts and behaviors are influenced by interactions with other people. They conduct research on a variety of topics including attitude formation and change, persuasion and conformity, attraction, group dynamics, and other interpersonal behaviors such as altruism and aggression. In addition to teaching and research, they design and evaluate policy and programs in diverse areas such as education, conflict resolution, and environmental protection.

Social psychologists contribute knowledge to a number of fields including health, business, law, the environment, education, and politics. They work in a number of settings including academic institutions, advertising agencies, business, health-care settings, and government agencies.

SPORTS PSYCHOLOGY

Sports psychology is the scientific study of psychological factors associated with participation and performance in sports. Sports psychologists are interested in understanding how participation in sports affects an individual's psychological development, health, and well-being. Sports psychologists often help athletes to improve their performance in competition, improve their motivation, cope with the pressures of competition (including anxiety and fear of failure), adjust to injury and transition out of competitive sports, and deal with life issues that affect their ability to focus and achieve optimal performance in their sport. Other services provided to individuals and groups include assistance with exercise adherence, communication, teamwork, program development, and program evaluation. Similar to other subfields of psychology, professionals in this area are service providers, researchers, and teachers. Some sports psychologists work for professional sports teams, many as a part of an independent sports psychology consulting practice. Others work in university counseling centers or teach in colleges or universities.

Other Helping Professions

PSYCHIATRY

Psychiatry is a medical discipline that is concerned with the origin, diagnosis, prevention, and treatment of mental illnesses including substance abuse and addiction. It integrates biological, psychological, and social aspects of mental health to provide medical care for a range of mental, emotional, and behavioral difficulties. Therefore, psychiatrists are uniquely qualified to assess both the mental and physical aspects of psychological disturbances. Most psychiatrists work with the seriously mentally ill. Many of their patients require medication as a part of their treatment. Psychiatrists are often involved in emergency and crisis evaluation and intervention and work with patients in both inpatient and outpatient settings.

Psychiatry and psychology have some essential differences in training. Psychiatrists earn a medical degree, which means that they complete 4 years of medical school and 3 years of residency training in psychiatry.

Many also complete a 1- or 2-year fellowship in psychiatry. Their medical training prepares them to understand the complex relationship between emotional and other medical illnesses and to evaluate medical and psychological data, make diagnoses, and develop treatment plans. Therefore, unlike psychologists, whose training focuses mainly on behavior and mental processes, psychiatrists obtain training that covers all body systems and disease processes and generally follows the medical model of biological causes to illness and disease, including mental illness. Psychology training takes a broader focus on the environments in which people live, including culture and context (e.g., socioeconomic, geographical, political). Practical training for psychologists (i.e., practicum and predoctoral internship) focuses intensely on psychological assessment, prevention, and psychotherapy. Psychologists use a variety of standardized psychological tests to assess emotional functioning, intelligence, and personality, while psychiatry residency programs typically focus on patient evaluation for medication and hospitalization and less on psychotherapy.

With few exceptions, psychiatrists are the only mental health professionals who can prescribe medication and admit and discharge patients from the hospital. Currently a couple of states allow psychologists to have limited privileges to prescribe medication. Similar to psychologists, many psychiatrists specialize in a particular developmental age range, such as child, adult, or geriatric psychiatry, or on a focused area of practice, such as forensic psychiatry, emergency psychiatry, or neuropsychiatry. In addition to clinical settings (e.g., hospitals, clinics, and private practices), some psychiatrists are administrators and lead multidisciplinary teams. Others psychiatrists are primarily involved in research and training. The median annual income in 2005 for a psychiatrist with more than 1 year in the specialty was $180,000 (U. S. Bureau of Labor Statistics, n.d.).

SOCIAL WORK

Social workers are mental health professionals who typically work to enhance the well-being of individuals, families, groups, and communities. Social workers help to meet the basic needs of all people and empower those who are vulnerable, oppressed, or living in poverty. They help people to identify and manage situations that contribute to problems in living. A defining feature of social work is the profession's dual focus on the individual in a social context and on the betterment of society. In addition to assisting individuals, they are advocates for change. As such, they are involved in public policy, legislation, and social advocacy efforts.

The training social workers receive is very different from that of psychologists. Entry into the profession of social work requires only a master's

TABLE 1.1

Annual Median Salaries of Social Workers in 2004

Specialty area	Median salary
Child, family, and school	$34,820
Medical and public health	$40,080
Mental health and substance abuse	$33,920
All others[a]	$39,440

Note. From U.S. Bureau of Labor Statistics (n.d.).
[a]Includes individual and family services and those employed by local and state government.

degree, not a doctoral degree as for psychology. The coursework required for a master's degree in social work often focuses on systems (including family and community systems) and administration, whereas coursework in psychology focuses more on individual mental processes. Social work is not typically considered a scientific discipline, as is psychology. Therefore, most social work graduate programs do not integrate scientific research findings and practice to the same extent that psychology programs do. Given the longer, more intensive study required of doctoral work, the doctoral degree in psychology affords more opportunities for supervised clinical training experiences.

Social workers are employed in a variety of settings such as schools, family service and public health agencies, child welfare agencies, homeless shelters, hospitals, employee assistance programs, and private practice. The median annual earnings of social workers vary slightly by industry, as displayed in Table 1.1.

COUNSELING

Counselors are master's level mental health practitioners who work with people to promote healthy functioning in the family, school, and community. Types of counselors include mental health counselors, community agency counselors, and school counselors. Mental health and community agency counselors are trained to help people cope with emotional and mental illnesses, addictions, and difficulties in life transitions (such as coping with illness or divorce). School counselors work with children in school settings to address emotional and social problems that interfere with the child's ability to learn. They also work with students to help them to see the connection between what they are learning in school and the jobs that may be of interest to them in the future. High school counselors focus on career planning by helping students learn more about themselves (e.g., interests, skills, abilities), opportunities for higher edu-

TABLE 1.2

Annual Median Salaries of Counselors in 2004

Specialty area	Median salary
Educational, vocational, and school	$45,570
Substance abuse and behavioral	$32,960
Rehabilitation	$27,870
Marriage and family	$38,980

Note. Data from U.S. Bureau of Labor Statistics (n.d.).

cation (college, and graduate and professional schools), and future jobs and careers.

Counseling training differs from that of psychology in a number of ways. Psychologists are required to take general or core psychology courses (e.g., biological bases of behavior, history and systems of psychology, social psychology, individual differences) that are not required in counseling programs. Psychotherapy and psychological assessment training also is more extensive in doctoral psychology programs. Most master's level counseling programs require a year of part-time internship experience, whereas doctoral psychology programs require 2 years of part-time practicum experience and 1 year of full-time internship experience. In general, psychology programs have a greater focus on research and the integration of research with practice than do counseling programs. Psychology doctoral programs typically require that students engage in independent research and complete a research dissertation.

Counselors work in a variety of settings, including educational, health care, legal, residential, private practice, and community agency settings. The median annual earnings of counselors vary by industry. See Table 1.2 for a breakdown of median annual salaries by specialty area.

Current and Future Trends in Psychology

Psychology is a dynamic field that keeps pace with social, economic, and political changes and scientific and technological advances. Some of the contemporary advances in psychology that have integrated interdisciplinary approaches to the study of human behavior include cognitive neuroscience and molecular biology, genetics, computer technology, health science and health care policy, homeland security and disaster response, and positive psychology. The current and future trends in each of these areas are discussed next.

COGNITIVE NEUROSCIENCE AND MOLECULAR BIOLOGY

Psychology is now expanding its boundaries to overlap with *neuroscience* (a subfield of biology that studies the brain and nervous system) and *molecular biology* (a subfield of biology that studies the structure and function of biological molecules such as DNA). *Cognitive neuroscience* is the study of cognitive processes using the methods and findings from neuroscience. Using advanced brain-imaging techniques, psychologists and neuroscientists are studying different mechanisms involved in cognitions and behavior. Technologies such as fMRI—in which radio waves and a strong magnetic field are used to provide clear and detailed pictures of the brain—and other brain imaging techniques are providing increasingly high-resolution maps of large-scale neural activity. All of these technological advances are bringing scientists closer to discovering how neurons, shaped by interactions between genes and the environment, give rise to behavior (Benson, 2004).

How people perceive the touch, emotions, and pain of others, as well as the behavioral intention of others is the focus of study for some psychologists interested in the brain and behavior, linking the fields of cognitive neuroscience and molecular biology. Have you ever seen people stub their toe or bump their head on something and wince as if you felt their pain? Research that uses neuroimaging has identified a set of neurons called *mirror neurons* that could help explain why people empathize with others and how they learn through mimicry. Mirror neurons are a type of brain cell that responds equally whether we perform an action or witness someone else perform the same action. Some suggest that mirror neurons might even help explain autism and the evolution of language (Winerman, 2005a).

Psychologists, neurologists, and other medical professionals are currently exploring ways to better understand and improve the brain's functioning at work by studying mental workload and vigilance. One goal of this work is to find ways to anticipate cognitive decline or fatigue in workers to prevent human error and safety problems (Huff, 2004). The latest neuroimaging techniques such as fMRI, near-infrared spectroscopy (in which laser optics are used to measure brain functioning), and PET (in which images are based on the detection of radiation from the emission of tiny particles emitted from a radioactive substance administered to the patient) are being used in the lab to study how the brain learns and processes information during tasks such as piloting a simulated flight or driving an automobile. This line of research could have implications for a range of work settings, including those of air traffic controllers, airport baggage screeners, and assembly-line workers. For example, one research team monitors participants' brain activity with electroencephalograph measurements while performing a simulated flight task to study cognitive decline and fatigue to prevent safety problems (Huff, 2004).

GENETICS

Rapid advances in technology have also led to some of the most exciting new discoveries about the brain and human genomes. For example, in 2000 a working draft mapping of the human genetic code was completed, which provided a research basis for a new understanding of human development and disease. Behavioral genetics continues to hold promise for a better understanding of the biological basis of behavior. Recent research continues to reinforce that to understand behavior and mental health, one must understand not only behavior and genetics in isolation but also how they work together and how genes interact with the environment. New research techniques from molecular biology are providing scientists with the means to directly manipulate genes in animals and to observe the altered genes' effects on behavior (Benson, 2004).

COMPUTER TECHNOLOGY

Modern technological advances are also affecting psychological assessment and treatment, including psychophysiological assessment and biofeedback, computer-based assessment, and virtual reality treatments. For example, some psychologists are using virtual reality together with cognitive–behavioral therapy as a tool to treat phobias such as the fear of flying (Winerman, 2005b). Three-dimensional computer graphics simulate environments and situations in the real world to help clients overcome their fears. This treatment, based on the principles of exposure, allows the therapist to carefully introduce and control the amount of exposure to the feared object in each session. Psychologists are using virtual reality so that clients with a fear of flying can experience "virtual" flights via a video screen in a helmet and vibrating chair (Winerman, 2005b). Clients see an image of the inside of an airplane on the screen inside the helmet. Sensors on the helmet pick up head movements so that when the person turns his or her head, the view changes accordingly. This process simulates looking around the inside of the plane, out the window, and across the aisle. The earphones provide an audio of the flight attendants and the pilot making announcements. The chair vibrates to simulate the feel of engines, turbulence, or descending landing gear (Winerman, 2005b). Other psychologists have used virtual reality to treat people with other fears, such as fears of spiders, heights, storms, and public speaking (Winerman, 2005b).

The advantages of this new treatment are convenience and confidentiality. It offers clients an experience that is more realistic than imagery and more convenient and private than real life exposure. Clients do not have to worry about running into people they know and disclosing or explaining their treatment to others. Clinicians can also carefully control the amount of exposure in each treatment session. Reports have suggested that it is easier to get clients to agree to exposure therapy when it begins virtually rather than in real life.

HEALTH SCIENCE AND HEALTH CARE POLICY

Psychology has responded to changes in U.S. health care and health care policy, including managed care, cost containment, and integrated delivery systems. For example, there is a growing demand for integrated, comprehensive health services that combine health care, behavior, prevention, health promotion, and disease management. In response to this need, psychologists are offering services beyond traditional psychotherapy and assessment by expanding into emerging practice areas (Clay, 2005). Given that chronic disease is often caused by behaviors such as smoking, poor diet, and inadequate exercise, psychologists are ideally situated to develop and implement behavioral intervention programs. A common recommendation from physicians is to "exercise and eat better." Psychologists understand and can intervene to get people to change their behavior (Kersting, 2005).

HOMELAND SECURITY AND DISASTER RESPONSE

Another contemporary area in which psychologists are expanding their practice is in homeland security and in response to terrorism and natural disasters. For example, psychologists in the field of deception detection consult with the U.S. Department of Homeland Security and other federal agencies (such as the Central Intelligence Agency) to seek new techniques to determine the difference between factual and fabricated information provided to the government regarding threats to national security. Other psychological research on persuasion and compliance may be particularly helpful in studying terrorism (Dingfelder, 2004). Disaster relief efforts also continue to be a growing area of practice and outreach activities for psychologists.

Psychological interventions go beyond immediate crisis intervention for disasters. Stress and anxiety are often experienced for months or years after such trauma. Psychologists work with people as they rebuild their homes, lives, and businesses. For example, I/O psychologists assist business leaders with strategies to help their businesses survive, to support employees who may have lost their houses or family members, and to adapt to a changing workforce and understaffing (Dingfelder, 2006a). Other psychologists help social service workers so that these workers do not lose sight of their own needs, teaching them about the toll that chronic stress takes on the body and mind and the importance of stress management and relaxation (Dingfelder, 2006b).

POSITIVE PSYCHOLOGY

Positive psychology concerns the study of what makes people happy or facilitates a sense of well-being. Psychologists interested in this area of psychology generally study subjective experiences such as happiness and optimism, personality traits (such as wisdom and courage), and the social structures that help to promote feelings of happiness. The underlying assumption of positive psychology is that enhancing positive emotions helps to promote well-being, personal growth, and optimal functioning.

Summary

It is probably becoming evident just how broad and useful the field of psychology really is. Psychology's dual focus on research and practice adds synergy to an already dynamic and multifaceted discipline. Contemporary trends in psychology have kept pace with technological advances and global changes. Psychology continues to expand its boundaries by intersecting with neuroscience and health science, and by integrating cross-disciplinary research. As you begin to see all that psychology has to offer, have a look in the following chapters at where it can take you as a student of psychology.

Suggested Web Sites

- American Psychological Association (APA). This is the Web site for the largest professional organization for psychologists: http://www.apa.org
- APA Divisions. This page provides links to the home pages of the divisions of APA, which represent some of the many subfields of psychology and areas of interest: http://www.apa.org/about/division.html

- APA Resources for Students. This page provides useful information for students, including what you need to know to become a psychologist: http://www.apa.org/students/
- APA Careers for the Twenty-First Century. This page provides information about psychology, its subfields, and job outlook. It also provides information related to the type of work that psychologists do and the settings in which they work; APA resources for students are also provided. See http://www.apa.org/topics/psychologycareer.html
- gradPSYCH Career Center. Find your niche in psychology through this directory of creative career tracks: http://www.gradpsych.apags.org/career.html
- Psychology in the News. This site provides current press releases relevant to the science and practice of psychology: http://www.psycport.com/
- Psych Web. This Web site contains lots of psychology-related information for students: http://www.psywww.com/index.html
- Psi Chi: The National Honor Society in Psychology. This Web site includes articles relevant to studying psychology as an undergraduate and other interesting contemporary information about psychology: http://www.psichi.org/
- National Association of School Psychologists. This is the Web site of the national professional association for school psychologists and contains current information about the field: http://www.nasponline.org/
- American Counseling Association. This is the Web site of the national professional organization for counselors and contains useful contemporary information about the profession: http://www.counseling.org
- National Association of Social Workers. This Web site of the national professional organization for social workers provides information relevant to the field: http://www.naswca.org/
- American Psychiatric Association. This Web site of the national association for psychiatrists provides information about the profession of psychiatry: http://www.psych.org

Suggested Reading

Backman, L., & von Hofsten, C. (Eds.). (2002). *Psychology at the turn of the millennium: Cognitive, biological , and health perspectives* (Vol. 1). New York: Taylor & Francis.

Coleman, A. (1999). *What is psychology?* (3rd ed.). New York: Routledge.

Kuther, T. L. (2006). *The psychology major's handbook* (2nd ed.). Belmont, CA: Thomson.

Snyder, C. R., & Ingram, R. E. (Eds.). (2000). *Handbook of psychological change: Psychotherapy processes & practices for the 21st century.* New York: Wiley.

Snyder, C. R., & Lopez, S. J. (Eds.). (2002). *Handbook of positive psychology.* New York: Oxford University Press.

von Hofsten, C., & Backman, L. (Eds.). (2002). *Psychology at the turn of the millennium: Social, developmental, and clinical perspectives* (Vol. 2). New York: Taylor & Francis.

What Is an Undergraduate Major in Psychology All About?

2

W hat can you expect as an undergraduate psychology major? The many skills and abilities you can develop as a psychology major include scientific problem-solving skills, analytic and research skills, and interpersonal and communication skills. The psychology major is an excellent choice for the development of skills and abilities that transfer readily to other fields of study or work.

What to Expect: Typical Requirements for a Major in Psychology

Most psychology departments require some combination of lecture and laboratory or practical experience courses. In addition, most undergraduate programs require a combination of science and liberal arts courses. Sound scientific training is fundamental to the undergraduate major in psychology. As a psychology major, you can expect rigorous training in the scientific method and statistics. Many students are surprised by this. It is common to think of psychology as a field that is concerned with helping people, which it is. However, psychology also is very much a scientific discipline.

In general, you can probably expect a core group of psychology lecture courses and another group of psychology courses that students can choose as electives. Some of the most common courses are described later in the chapter. Elective courses are often run as seminars with smaller groups of more advanced students. Upper level or advanced seminars provide an opportunity for intensive study on a particular topic.

Some psychology departments require laboratory courses in which the student practices experimental research or observes phenomena. Laboratory courses offer hands-on experience and the opportunity to see firsthand what you have learned about in other classes. Through laboratory experience, students become familiar with ethical standards for research (discussed later in the chapter), the scientific method, and writing laboratory or research reports.

To provide students with practical experience, some departments offer courses that require field experiences or internships. Field experiences provide real-world job-related learning experiences as well as the opportunity to observe psychologists and other mental health professionals at work. They also provide students with the opportunity to put to use what they have learned in the classroom. Typical settings for practical experiences include schools and day care centers, nursing homes, hospitals, community centers, residential treatment facilities for emotionally disturbed children, battered women's shelters, and suicide hotlines.

Thesis and senior projects are sometimes required but most often are offered as optional courses for advanced students who plan to graduate with honors or are considering graduate training in psychology. Completing a thesis or senior project offers you the opportunity to initiate your own research project or work closely with a faculty member engaged in ongoing research. Undergraduate research experience is often beneficial in the admissions process for graduate study in psychology. This is discussed in more depth in chapters 6 and 9, this volume.

Courses and Topics of Study

Gathering information about the curriculum is an important step toward making a decision about whether psychology is the right major for you. Although every college and university has its own unique set of required courses and prerequisites, and the exact titles of courses may vary, you can expect some consistency and predictability across institutions. For example, almost every undergraduate psychology department requires students to begin their course of study with an introductory course that provides an overview of the field, its history and development, major subfields and theories, and an introduction to the scientific method and statistics.

Following the introductory course, a number of courses are generally required of most psychology majors, which are often referred to as part of the core curriculum. Given that the discipline of psychology is strongly rooted in the scientific tradition of research and the scientific method, almost all psychology departments require a research methods course and a statistics course as part of the core curriculum. The courses in Table 2.1 were found to be offered most frequently across institutions (Stoloff, Sanders, & McCarthy, 2005).

In addition to required psychology courses, students are typically asked to choose additional courses to fit their individual interests and goals, which are usually referred to as *electives*. Sample elective courses and their descriptions are offered in Table 2.2.

Ethical Issues for Undergraduate Psychology Students

Psychologists build their professional and scientific work on a common set of ethical principles and standards. Psychologists must consider the American Psychological Association's (APA's) Ethics Code in addition to applicable laws and psychology board regulations when making decisions regarding their professional behavior. The goal of this code is the welfare and protection of the individuals and groups with whom psychologists work and the education of APA members, students, and the public regarding ethical standards. As an undergraduate psychology major, you will likely encounter ethical concepts in one or more of your courses. It is important to be familiar with the APA Ethics Code and to be knowledgeable about how it applies to you as an undergraduate student of psychology. The General Principles from the "Ethical Principles of Psychologists and Code of Conduct" (American Psychological Association, 2002) is provided in Exhibit 2.1. The complete Ethics Code is available online at http://www.apa.org/ethics/homepage.html.

You may want to conduct independent research or to work as a part of a faculty member's research team. As a student researcher, you must follow proper procedures with regard to the ethical treatment of human and animal research participants. Researchers must ask themselves whether the potential benefits of the research outweigh the potential harm or costs to the participant. One way to minimize the cost or harm

TABLE 2.1

Sample Required Psychology Courses

Course name	Course description
Introduction to psychology	Overview of the field and often a prerequisite for all other courses in psychology.
Research methods	Overview of different types of experiments, how to design research, and ethical issues involved in research.
Introduction to statistics	Overview on how to apply descriptive and inferential statistics to analyze and interpret experimental results.
Abnormal psychology	Overview of the major psychological disorders, their causes, and treatments.
Social psychology	Theory and method of social psychology including impression formation, social cognition, attitude change, social influence, and group processes.
Theories of personality	Major theories of personality, with an emphasis on how personality influences behavior.
Cognitive psychology	Mental processes including memory, perception, thinking, and language.
Physiological psychology	Overview of neurobiological bases of behavior, including neurons and neurotransmitters. Brain anatomy and functioning, including technological advances in brain imaging.
History and systems of psychology	Development of psychology and its systems of thought as a function of philosophical and scientific antecedents.
Developmental psychology	Overview of cognitive, social, emotional, moral, and physical development from birth through old age.

to human participants is to obtain *informed consent* prior to participation. This means that the researcher, in the process of obtaining potential participants' consent to participate, must fully inform them about the nature of the research and all possible risks and benefits. Informed consent is only one of the ethical issues that must be considered in conducting research with human participants. Students involved in research should seek guidance on how to apply the Ethics Code across all aspects of the research process.

Skills in ethical decision making are transferable to areas outside of psychology. Concepts learned about the process of gathering information and making judgments and decisions can be useful in many life contexts and job settings. For example, people working in business, industry, and community settings are often confronted with making sound ethical choices.

TABLE 2.2

Sample Elective Psychology Courses

Course name	Course description
Psychology of learning	Overview of learning processes, including habituation and sensitization, conditioning, contingencies of reinforcement and discrimination, and concept formation.
Industrial/organizational psychology	Introduction to the methods used by industrial/organizational psychologists to increase organizational effectiveness and individual well-being.
Child psychology	Child biological, motor, perceptual, cognitive, language, emotional, social, and gender development.
Adolescent psychology	Overview of adolescent development, peer and family influences, and personal adjustment.
Adulthood and aging	Theoretical perspectives on aging and changes in cognitive, social, and personality functioning.
Psychological measurement	Measurement theory and the construction, administration, and interpretation of psychological tests of personality, intelligence, and abilities.
Sensation and perception	Human sensory and perceptual processes with applications to psychological issues.
Human sexuality	Overview of theory, research, and practice in the area of human sexuality. Attitudes, beliefs, and feelings about sexuality.
Health psychology	Impact of behavior, cognition, and affect on health and wellness, coping styles, and the prevention and treatment of disease.
Psychology of women	Women's issues from a psychological perspective, reexamining traditional psychological theories, sex differences, and sex-role socialization.
Educational psychology	Overview of learning processes in educational settings, with an emphasis on learning challenges, motivation, educational assessment, and classroom management.
Experimental psychology	Major empirical findings and research strategies in the scientific study of psychology.
Cross-cultural psychology	Similarities and differences in human behavior across different cultures. Identifies different psychological constructs and explanatory models used by various cultures.
Clinical or counseling psychology	Introduction to the professional practice of psychology, including assessment, intervention, work settings, and professional issues.

EXHIBIT 2.1

General Principles From the "American Psychological Association Ethical Principles of Psychologists and Code of Conduct" (2002)

This section consists of General Principles. General Principles, as opposed to Ethical Standards, are aspirational in nature. Their intent is to guide and inspire psychologists toward the very highest ethical ideals of the profession. General Principles, in contrast to Ethical Standards, do not represent obligations and should not form the basis for imposing sanctions. Relying upon General Principles for either of these reasons distorts both their meaning and purpose.

Principle A: Beneficence and Nonmaleficence

Psychologists strive to benefit those with whom they work and take care to do no harm. In their professional actions, psychologists seek to safeguard the welfare and rights of those with whom they interact professionally and other affected persons, and the welfare of animal subjects of research. When conflicts occur among psychologists' obligations or concerns, they attempt to resolve these conflicts in a responsible fashion that avoids or minimizes harm. Because psychologists' scientific and professional judgments and actions may affect the lives of others, they are alert to and guard against personal, financial, social, organizational, or political factors that might lead to misuse of their influence. Psychologists strive to be aware of the possible effect of their own physical and mental health on their ability to help those with whom they work.

Principle B: Fidelity and Responsibility

Psychologists establish relationships of trust with those with whom they work. They are aware of their professional and scientific responsibilities to society and to the specific communities in which they work. Psychologists uphold professional standards of conduct, clarify their professional roles and obligations, accept appropriate responsibility for their behavior, and seek to manage conflicts of interest that could lead to exploitation or harm. Psychologists consult with, refer to, or cooperate with other professionals and institutions to the extent needed to serve the best interests of those with whom they work. They are concerned about the ethical compliance of their colleagues' scientific and professional conduct. Psychologists strive to contribute a portion of their professional time for little or no compensation or personal advantage.

Principle C: Integrity

Psychologists seek to promote accuracy, honesty, and truthfulness in the science, teaching, and practice of psychology. In these activities psychologists do not steal, cheat, or engage in fraud, subterfuge, or intentional misrepresentation of fact. Psychologists strive to keep their promises and to avoid unwise or unclear commitments. In situations in which deception may be ethically justifiable to maximize benefits and minimize harm, psychologists have a serious obligation to consider the need for, the possible consequences of, and their responsibility to correct any resulting mistrust or other harmful effects that arise from the use of such techniques.

Principle D: Justice

Psychologists recognize that fairness and justice entitle all persons to access to and benefit from the contributions of psychology and to equal quality in the processes, procedures, and services being conducted by psychologists. Psychologists exercise reasonable judgment and take precautions to ensure that their potential biases, the boundaries of their competence, and the limitations of their expertise do not lead to or condone unjust practices.

Principle E: Respect for People's Rights and Dignity

Psychologists respect the dignity and worth of all people, and the rights of individuals to privacy, confidentiality, and self-determination. Psychologists are aware that special safeguards may be necessary to protect the rights and welfare of persons or communities whose vulnerabilities impair autonomous decision-making. Psychologists are aware of and respect cultural, individual, and role differences, including those based on age, gender, gender identity, race, ethnicity, culture, national origin, religion, sexual orientation, disability, language, and socioeconomic status and consider these factors when working with members of such groups. Psychologists try to eliminate the effect on their work of biases based on those factors, and they do not knowingly participate in or condone activities of others based upon such prejudices.

Note. From "Ethical Principles of Psychologists and Code of Conduct," by the American Psychological Association, 2002, *American Psychologist, 57*, 1062–1063. Copyright 2002 by the American Psychological Association. Available at http://www.apa.org/ethics/homepage.html

Psychology: A Good Choice for the Development of Transferable Skills and Abilities

As a psychology major you will learn many valuable skills that will help you to succeed in whatever career path you choose. You will acquire a host of transferable skills that will open up a world of possibilities for you! The combination of liberal arts and science makes the psychology major distinctive. A liberal arts education exposes students to a variety of disciplines and is great preparation for lifelong learning, critical thinking, and action emphasizing specialized and general knowledge and skills (McGovern, Furumoto, Halpern, Kimble, & McKeachie, 1991). For example, courses in literature, history, and the arts will help you to learn how to analyze things for yourself and to think independently. The scientific aspect of psychology prepares students to use investigative skills to gather and synthesize information.

Transferable skills are those that are useful beyond any given curriculum and across a wide variety of settings, situations, and jobs. These are the skills that are attractive to employers. Exhibit 2.2 summarizes some of the qualities, skills, and abilities ranked most important by employers (Appleby, 2000). Think about it. All of these traits involve skills typical of psychology majors: working well with people both individually and in groups, communicating effectively, solving problems, and influencing others.

Many psychology courses (e.g., abnormal psychology, social psychology, and multicultural psychology) present diverse perspectives and theories for understanding people's behavior, attitudes, and communication patterns. Exposure to diverse perspectives helps students to develop a flexible awareness of individual differences and encourages them to become more self-aware and better communicators. In addition, courses in research and statistics will give you the skills you need to analyze and interpret data and to make decisions. As you can see, the skills you will learn as a psychology major are highly valued.

Although many of the skills listed in Exhibit 2.2 can be learned through formal coursework, much of your potential can only be realized through self-discipline and persistent effort that only you can provide. Putting extra effort into your coursework can facilitate the development of some skills. Others are better learned outside of the classroom by seeking out challenging opportunities, gaining life experiences, building confidence in your abilities, and developing an orientation to lifelong learning. Thus, you are the one who is ultimately in control of realizing your full poten-

EXHIBIT 2.2

Skills Nurtured in a Psychology Curriculum

Demonstrates good interpersonal skills

Displays good problem solving skills

Works productively as a member of a team

Has high ethical standards

Listens carefully and accurately

Speaks articulately and persuasively

Writes clearly and precisely

Thinks logically and creatively

Is able to gather and organize information from multiple sources

Displays computer literacy

Exhibits good research and statistical skills

Note. From "Job Skills Valued by Employers Who Interview Psychology Majors," by D. Appleby, 2000, *Eye on Psi Chi, 4*(3), p. 17. Copyright 2000 by Psi Chi, the National Honor Society in Psychology (http://www.psichi.org). Adapted with permission. All rights reserved.

tial. Chapter 6 (this volume) will get you started by suggesting some tips on how you can get the most out of your psychology major.

How Do I Find the Best Undergraduate Psychology Program?

In addition to general considerations in choosing a college or university (e.g., geographical location, cost, university environment), there are several other important factors to consider when choosing an undergraduate program in psychology. Web sites of undergraduate psychology departments are a good place to begin to get an overview of the program and available resources and opportunities for students. While visiting a college or university, visit the psychology department, talk to faculty and students, and get a feel for whether or not it is a place where you would feel comfortable studying for the next 4 years. Visit some psychology classes to get a sense of faculty–student interactions, how challenging the courses are, and how active and involved the students are. Find out what activities, clubs, honor societies, and organizations the psychology department supports and the level of student interest in these organizations. Explore the availability of field experiences and observational learning as well. Many programs incorporate field experiences into coursework, whereas others have whole courses devoted to practical experience or internship. Look for established relationships between psychology department faculty and community agencies and organizations. These are all resources that will help you to get the most out of your undergraduate psychology degree.

If you are interested in going to graduate school, pay particular attention to the research opportunities for undergraduates, including opportunities to present the results of research at professional conferences. Ask about the research interests of the faculty and determine how good of a fit their interests are with yours. Research experience is an important factor in gaining admission to graduate study in psychology. The more closely you work with faculty, the more likely it will be that they will get to know you well enough to write a favorable letter of recommendation for your graduate school application. To learn more about graduate study, refer to chapter 9, this volume.

What About Online Learning?

Online instruction is an exciting new medium for the exchange of ideas and resources that continues to gain popularity. Some institutions specialize in online instruction, whereas other colleges and universities integrate it as an optional course format in addition to traditional face-to-face course delivery. According to a report of the APA Task Force on Distance Education and Training in Professional Psychology (2002), more than half of all regionally accredited colleges and universities offer courses or full degree programs through distance learning. The primary difference between traditional classroom-based instruction and online instruction is the way you get your information and how you interact with your instructors and classmates. How will you know if online learning is really for you? Success with online learning depends in part on your lifestyle and in part on a number of individual factors. Many people find that the flexibility of learning on a schedule that meets their personal needs and lifestyle is preferable to having a set class meeting time. With *asynchronous communication* (i.e., when students and the instructor do not have to be logged on at the same time to communicate because messages and information are posted and saved on the Web site), students can log on to the course Web site anytime (i.e., 24 hours a day, 7 days a week), anywhere (provided that Internet access is available).

Successful online learners typically possess key traits that are conducive to online learning. If you are thinking about enrolling in an online course as an easy way to earn credit, think again! Successful online learners are self-directed; motivated; comfortable working on computers; and able to use e-mail, Internet browsers, and word processors. They like to read and write; are inquisitive, self-disciplined, and independent; and are able to stay on task for long periods of time. Only you can be responsible for structuring your time in an online course.

Although online courses are incredibly convenient, they have a few disadvantages. Some students miss the face-to-face contact with other students and their professor. Interpersonal interaction can be particularly important in certain psychology courses, such as courses in helping skills, when it might be beneficial to learn how to incorporate verbal and nonverbal communication in the skills you are learning. In other courses, such as statistics, it might be reassuring to sit with the instructor to work through problems together. Other disadvantages include the frustrations that sometimes occur when using computer equipment and software. Perhaps the greatest potential downside of online instruction is that there is little to no opportunity to conduct research and interact one on one with faculty members. This could present a big disadvantage when applying to graduate school or a job. Gaining experience and developing relationships with faculty members help to ensure that you will have someone to go to for a letter of recommendation.

Although you will not have face-to-face contact with your instructor and classmates, online interaction is essential to online learning. Given that writing is the primary mode of communication, you should feel comfortable expressing your thoughts, opinions, and questions in written form. To succeed in an online class, you also need to feel comfortable initiating online communication with your instructor and fellow classmates. It is particularly important to feel comfortable asking questions, so that your instructor and classmates know when you are stuck and need help. Online discussions are analogous to discussions in class, thus they are a vital part of every course. They reflect your understanding of the material, as well as your ability to think critically, reflectively integrate learning material, and constructively engage your peers in thoughtful dialogue.

You can probably see by now that learning about yourself is one step toward making good decisions about your education and your future. You will learn even more about effective decision-making strategies in chapter 3, this volume.

What Challenges Lie Ahead?

Even if you are well on your way to deciding that psychology is definitely the right major for you, your journey has only just begun. Choosing a college major is only one decision among many that you will confront on your educational and career path. As you have already seen, many institutions offer a variety of psychology courses, leaving many choices up to you. All undergraduate students are assigned an advisor in their major, to whom they can turn for assistance and advice on course selection and available opportunities. As you progress in your studies, you will not only need to make choices about which electives to take, but you also will need to decide which opportunities to explore and take advantage of. It is well known that there is an *overt educational curriculum* (i.e., formal coursework) and a *covert curriculum* (i.e., learning that occurs outside of formal coursework and book knowledge; Appleby, 2000). An example of the covert curriculum is learning to be a leader through the experience of taking on a leadership role (e.g., president or chair) in your department's psychology club. The benefits that you derive from the covert curriculum are largely up to you.

One of the biggest challenges facing undergraduate psychology students is managing the workload and making the most of class lectures and study time. Even the most prepared students can find themselves feeling a little stressed and anxious when faced with organizing their time and coursework. Chapter 5 offers tips for how to manage the anxiety that often accompanies stressful situations like managing your time and choosing a college major.

Psychology as a Major?

I hope by now you have a lot of information to consider in deciding whether psychology is the right major for you. You may feel a bit overwhelmed with the amount of information presented in this chapter. Take some time to let it all sink in. Think about how the information presented here relates to what you are reading in your courses, what your instructors are saying, and what your fellow classmates are talking about. Do some soul searching. Which kinds of activities and challenges do you really enjoy and look forward to? Chapter 3 gives you some strategies for learning more about yourself and the world of work in psychology. It also offers some tips on decision-making strategies, so read on!

Suggested Web Sites

- APA Resources for Students. This page provides useful information for students, including what you need to know to become a psychologist: http://www.apa.org/students/

■ Strategies for Success for Distance Learners. This Web site provides tips for success for distance learners: http://www.worldwidelearn. com/education-articles/distance-learning-success.htm

■ Distance Learning in Psychology. This Web site provides links related to distance learning, including degree programs in psychology, Web-based courses in psychology, megasites on distance learning, and more: http://www.socialpsychology.org/distance.htm

Suggested Reading

Landrum, R. E., & Davis, S. F. (2007). *The psychology major: Career options and strategies for success* (3rd ed.). Upper Saddle River, NJ: Pearson Prentice Hall.

Morgan, B. L., & Korschgen, A. J. (2002). *Majoring in psychology? Career options for psychology undergraduates* (2nd ed.). Boston: Allyn & Bacon.

O'Hara, S. (2005). *What can you do with a major in psychology? Real people, real jobs, real rewards.* Hoboken, NJ: Wiley.

Peterson, T. (2006). *Peterson's four-year colleges.* Lawrenceville, NJ: Author.

How Do I Know if Psychology Is a Good Match for Me?

3

Who are you? What do you want out of life? Out of your future job? Understanding yourself is crucial to choosing the right college major. So, how will you know if psychology is a good match for you? By taking a good hard look at yourself—including your dreams, interests, personality, skills and abilities, values, and preferences—you will develop the self-awareness you need to make the best-informed choice you can about your college major. The skills you will learn in this chapter, and in chapters 4 and 5, include self-exploration, decision making, and managing the anxiety that often accompanies the stress of making important life decisions like choosing a college major. Not only will reading these chapters help you to choose a college major now but it also will help you to develop the skills you will need in the future to make good career choices and other life decisions.

The purpose of this chapter is to promote self-exploration and exploration of the world of work in psychology, as a way to assist you in making an appropriate match between your interests and abilities and the requirements and tasks of various work environments. This chapter includes self-assessments and exercises designed to boost your knowledge and decision-making power. Strategies for successfully matching your interests and the world of work are provided, and the value of making a good match (with respect to job satisfaction, productivity, motivation, wellness, etc.) is emphasized.

Self-Exploration

There are many ways to learn more about your interests, abilities, personality, and the other factors that are important in making a good educational and career decision. A good way to begin this process is to reflect on your experiences in school and work as well as in your community and family. It is important to consider your interests by thinking about the activities and environments that you enjoy. Your preferences and *self-efficacy*, or self-confidence, also weigh in heavily on career decisions. The following sections provide guidance on how to learn more about all of these aspects of yourself.

EDUCATIONAL AND VOCATIONAL HISTORY

Reviewing your personal educational and vocational history is a good way to begin your journey. This might be even more relevant if you have already graduated and have been working for a while. Consider your family background, childhood and adolescent years, educational and work history, vocationally related activities, and your current educational and work situation. Use the Educational and Vocational History Questionnaire provided in Appendix 3.1 to facilitate this self-reflective process. Look for any patterns that emerge. If you begin to see themes related to working with and helping people, a curiosity about human behavior, or a preference toward working with ideas versus working with your hands or tools, you may want to look further into psychology.

INTERESTS

We usually like or are interested in those activities that we have had experience with. Consider the kinds of tasks, courses, and jobs that you have really liked. What are your favorite hobbies or leisure activities? What would you most like to spend the rest of your life doing? What really makes you happy? It is important to have a clear and detailed image of your likes and dislikes. The more detailed your awareness is, the better. So, take the time to really flesh out your images of what really excites you and gets you motivated.

Another way to consider your interests is to indulge yourself in an *occupational daydream*. What is an occupational daydream? Set aside time in a quiet, relaxing place and imagine in your mind's eye what your ideal job or career would be. What would be your absolutely ideal job? Indulge yourself in every detail. What would you be doing? Who would you be doing it with, or would you be doing it alone? Would you be outdoors or inside? What part of the world would you be in? Would you travel? If so, how much, with who, and where? Would you be working with your hands or on intellectual ideas and problems? As you can see, the details you can furnish are endless. Try not to let reality intrude on your daydream. After all, it is a dream. What is important though, is that in every dream you have there is some underlying theme or aspect that can help you to learn more about the actual occupation or career that would be right for you.

After you have imagined your dream jobs, try putting five of these occupations that you have daydreamed about on paper. Are there any themes that have emerged in your dream occupations? Are any or all of them real or achievable? What could you do to achieve one or more of these dreams? Is there anything getting in the way or preventing you from achieving your dreams?

There also are many formal ways to assess your interests. Have a look at the suggested Web sites at the end of this chapter for links to self-assessments. In chapter 4 you will learn even more about assessment tools used by career counselors to help you in the self-exploration process.

PERSONALITY

Understanding your unique personality will help you to choose the college major that is a good fit for you. Developing an awareness of who you are, your preferences, and how you interact with the world will help you to make a better choice of educational and occupational environments. Psychologists and counselors use a number of standardized personality assessment measures to assist people in learning more about themselves. If you decide to seek out a career counselor, you may have the opportunity to complete one of these assessments. In the meantime, there are other ways that you can learn more about your personality.

Journaling is a powerful way to engage in introspection and to learn more about your personality. It allows you a private, creative, and endless space to reflect on your experiences, interactions with others, thoughts and feelings, and just about anything of importance to you. Regularly writing in a journal can provide you with the opportunity to more clearly define who you are, what you want out of life, and how you want to accomplish your goals. Try reflecting on the best and most challenging aspects of each day, your most affirming and most conflicted relationships, and your most peaceful and tumultuous moments. Think about your style of interpersonal interactions and how you solve interpersonal conflicts, manage and express your emotions, and deal with ambiguity and change. Which environments do you feel most at home in, and which take you outside of your comfort zone? If you need further help to get started, each day try to reflect on one of the following questions devised by Combs (2000).

- What are the most important things in your life?
- What are the activities that you love and enjoy most today?
- What would be your ideal work environment today?
- How would you define success today?
- What might be your purpose or destiny?
- How do you want to be perceived by your friends? Coworkers? Parents? Significant others?
- What magazine would you most like to be featured in for your tremendous accomplishments in 10 years?
- What would you like to be the best at in the world?
- Who are your heroes and what is it about them that you most want to be like?
- What do you really think should be changed in the world?
- What do you most want to be remembered for at the end of your life?
- Whom do you envy, and what is it about them that you envy?

RIASEC SYSTEM

John Holland is a prominent *vocational psychologist* (a psychologist who studies work and work behaviors) who contends that career choice and adjustment represent an extension of one's personality. He believes that people express their interests and values through their work. Holland's (1997) theory states that most people and their corresponding work environments, can be loosely categorized into six types. These types, described below, include Realistic (R), Investigative (I), Artistic (A), Social (S), Enterprising (E), and Conventional (C). These types are often referred to as the *RIASEC system*. Holland uses a hexagon to represent this system, with each point of the hexagon representing one of the types. The basic premise of Holland's theory is that people who find themselves in educational and work environments that are similar to their personality type tend to be more satisfied, persistent, and successful in their work. Look closely at the six types described below. Most people find several types that describe themselves. Which Holland type do you think best describes you?

1. *Realistic.* Those with a Realistic personality type tend to enjoy manual, mechanical, or athletic activities and using machines, tools, and objects in their hobbies or work. They may be drawn to courses that are practical and that teach the use of mechanical

or physical skills and may tend to approach problems in a practical or problem-solving manner.

2. *Investigative.* Investigative types enjoy analytical or intellectual activities and learning by reading, study, or investigation. People of this type are often curious, like to work independently, and enjoy the challenge of solving mathematical and scientific problems. They are likely to enjoy courses in math, physics, chemistry, biology, and other physical or biological sciences.

3. *Artistic.* Artistic people like to engage in creative work in music, writing, performance, and sculpture. They tend to be expressive and imaginative and value originality and creativity. Artistic persons enjoy working in unstructured situations that allow for innovation.

4. *Social.* Those with a Social personality type enjoy working with others and helping people. They prefer to work in teams to forward group goals. Social types tend to be sensitive to the needs of others and value educational and social issues.

5. *Enterprising.* Those with the Enterprising type enjoy leading, selling, motivating, and persuading others. They tend to be self-confident, sociable, and assertive and like to take on leadership roles. Enterprising types tend to value power, status, and wealth.

6. *Conventional.* Those with a Conventional personality type enjoy working with things, numbers, or machines to meet precise standards. They are often structured, accurate, and detail oriented and have a good ability to follow rules and orders. Conventional types have strengths in clerical and numerical ability and enjoy solving straightforward problems.

People and environments cannot be purely categorized into one type. In practice, three types are assigned to reflect a person's strongest areas of interest. A person's top three types are listed in descending order, with one's strongest interest listed first. The first letter of each type is used to form a three-letter code. This code is referred to as a *Holland type* or *Holland code*. Therefore, a Holland code consists of three letters from the RIASEC system that best represent a person's top three areas of interest. For example, a social science teacher may hold the three-letter code of SEA (Social–Enterprising–Artistic). This means that he or she has strong Social interests, followed by Enterprising and Artistic interests.

Work environments and college majors also can be classified using Holland RIASEC codes according to the characteristics and requirements of the work setting. For example, Realistic environments include work settings that require physical activity and the use of tools and machines. Some Realistic work environments include factories, repair shops, and

EXHIBIT 3.1

Occupations and College Majors by Holland Personality Type

Sample occupations	Sample college majors
Realistic	
Carpenter	Electrical engineering
Cook	Animal care technology
Electrician	Aerospace engineering
Technician	Architecture
Auto mechanic	Criminal justice
Floral designer	Environmental studies
Plumber	Building construction
Investigative	
Chemist	Anthropology
Computer programmer	Astronomy
Drafter	Biochemistry
Medical laboratory technician	Biological sciences
Biologist	Chemistry
Physician	Computer science
Physician assistant	Geography
Veterinarian	Forestry
Artistic	
Advertising	Architecture
Architect	Commercial art
Writer	Interior design
Fine artist	Advertising
Photographer	Art history
Interior designer	Communications
Musician	English
Social	
Counselor	Psychology
Teacher	Audiology
Mental health worker	Nutrition
Nurse	Philosophy
Speech therapist	Religious studies
Librarian	Sociology
Politics	Special education
Psychologist	Human development

Enterprising	
Financial analyst	Banking and finance
Lawyer	Hospitality and tourism
Lobbyist	Business administration
Salesperson	Economics
Business manager	Industrial relations
Public relations specialist	Public administration
Travel agent	Broadcasting
Reporter	Journalism

Conventional	
Accountant	Accounting
Bookkeeper	Computer science
Bank employee	Mathematics
Data processing	Statistics
Office clerk	Finance
Mail clerk	Medical record technology
Court reporter	

Note. Data from North Carolina State Occupational Information Coordinating Committee (n.d.); see also Kuther (2006) and Sharf (2006).

farms. See Exhibit 3.1 for sample occupations and college majors by Holland type.

One way to assess your three-letter Holland code is to complete the Career Interests Game at the University of Missouri Web site (University of Missouri—Columbia, 2007). After completing the Career Interests Game, think about how similar your code is to your current educational and work environments or to the environments that you are considering entering. It is important to consider which points on the RIASEC hexagon you were more strongly drawn to. Points on the hexagon that are closest to each other are considered to be more similar to each other, and those that are the farthest apart from each other are thought to be the most dissimilar. Therefore, if in the Career Interests Game you were drawn to corners of the room that were close to each other, you may have an easier time finding environments in which your interests and personality can best be expressed. If you were drawn to corners of the room that were the furthest apart, you may be more challenged to find one work environment that is compatible with your interests and personality characteristics.

Psychologists tend to have the three-letter code SIA (Social–Investigative–Artistic). Therefore, if you tend to have social interests, are investigative or inquisitive in nature, and have an appreciation for art, you have expressed interests that are similar to those of many psychologists. This suggests that psychology might be a good match for you. Of course, if your three-letter Holland code does not include these types, that does not necessarily mean an undergraduate major in psychology would not be a good match. The point is, the more similar your three-letter code is to SIA, the more similar your interests are to doctoral level psychologists' interests. The more dissimilar your code is, the more dissimilar your interests are to psychologists' interests. Therefore, if your code is very dissimilar (e.g., RCE), you may want to explore majors and careers that are consistent with your code to see if your principal interests lie somewhere other than psychology. Remember, your results on any one assessment only give you a piece of information about yourself to help to point you in the right direction for further exploration. Always remember to look at the big picture, themes across various assessments, and your experiences.

The amount of experience you have had interacting in particular environments is an important consideration. In the Career Interests Game, you may have been drawn to particular corners of the room and not others as a result of your familiarity and comfort in various environments. This is important to consider because without relevant experience in a particular area you may be unlikely to pursue or explore college majors or jobs associated with that area. Sometimes you do not know whether you are going to like something until you try it. Once you try something, you are likely to gain more experience and skills in that area. Gaining more experience and skills in a particular area can increase your self-confidence as well as your interest. You may need to try exploring areas outside of your comfort zone and to gain additional experiences in areas that are new or unknown to you.

For more information, or for further assessment of your Holland type, try taking the Self-Directed Search (Holland, 1994; available online at http://www.self-directed-search.com). The Self-Directed Search is a self-report inventory designed to assess your three-letter Holland code to help you find the careers that best match your interests and abilities. A list of occupations with codes identical or similar to your own is available in *The Occupations Finder* (Holland, 2000). In addition, the *Educational Opportunities Finder* (Rosen, Holmberg, & Holland, 1994) lists more than 750 programs of study. Another good resource is the *Dictionary of Holland Occupational Codes* (Gottfredson & Holland, 1996), which lists more than 12,000 occupations.

MYERS–BRIGGS TYPE THEORY

The Myers–Briggs type theory has become popular with career counselors. This theory concerns the way that individuals observe the world and make decisions based on their perceptions (Myers, 1993). The theory is based on four bipolar categories that work in conjunction with each other and form the basis of the Myers–Briggs typology. Knowledge of your type will help you to learn more about your preferences. A basic understanding of these bipolar categories, representing eight preferences, provides an introduction to what this typology system has to offer.

- *Extraversion–Introversion.* This dichotomy refers to where people prefer to focus their attention and get their energy.
  - *Extraversion* refers to making perceptions and judgments in the outer world of people and objects. Extraverts prefer to take action and tend to be verbally and physically active. With regard to work environments and tasks, extraverts tend to prefer working with others.
  - *Introversion* refers to making perceptions and judgments based on one's interests in his or her inner world consisting of concepts and ideas. Introverts think long and hard before they act. They also tend to work and solve problems on their own.
- *Sensing–Intuition.*[1] There are two ways of taking in information.
  - *Sensing* refers to taking in information by using one's senses of vision, hearing, smelling, tasting, and touching. Sensing individuals typically focus their attention on events that happen immediately around them and often have a good memory for details.
  - *Intuition* relies on insight and the use of the unconscious to add ideas to external perceptions or observations. Thus, people with this type tend to perceive meanings and relationships in events.
- *Thinking–Feeling.* These are two contrasting modes of making decisions.
  - *Thinking* individuals typically are logical and objective with regard to analyzing an observed idea or event.
  - *Feeling* types frequently make judgments on the basis of the values applied to one's observations or ideas. People of this type are often concerned with the impact of their judgment or decision.
- *Judging–Perceiving.* This dichotomy refers to how individuals deal with the external world.
  - *Judging* individuals prefer to make decisions and live their lives in an organized manner.
  - *Perceiving* individuals prefer flexibility and keeping their options open.

Sixteen different types can result from the four dichotomies described above. The characteristics frequently associated with each type are pro-

---

[1]Because there are two "I"s in the Myers–Briggs system, Introversion and Intuition, the letter *N* is used to denote the Intuitive type.

vided in Myers (1998). Psychologists, counselors, and social workers frequently express preferences consistent with ENFP, exhibiting strengths in people skills, adaptability, and creativity (Hammer, 1993). Other frequent combinations for psychologists, counselors, and social workers include INFJ, INFP, and ENFJ. Therefore, many people working in these areas tend to report a preference for focusing on the big picture and patterns and meanings in data, and they are imaginative and verbally creative (N Type; Myers, 1998). They also tend to have preferences for using feelings in decision making and being empathic, compassionate, appreciative, and supportive of others (F type; Myers, 1998).

The Myers–Briggs Type Indicator (MBTI) manual (Myers, McCaulley, Quenk, & Hammer, 1998) cautioned that type definitions describe only general characteristics. People with the same type exhibit various differences. The MBTI yields scores on each of the four dichotomies. For those interested in a more formalized assessment of their Myers–Briggs type, refer to the Web site (http://www.capt.org/take-mbti-assessment/mbti.htm) or a career counselor.

SKILLS AND ABILITIES

Estimating your skills and abilities through an honest self-appraisal process is an important component of self-awareness. Spend time thinking about your strengths and the things you are good at. What makes you stand out in a crowd? Consider the jobs you have had and the courses you have taken so far. In which areas do you excel? For a quick estimate, complete the exercise in Appendix 3.2. Also, have a look at your responses on the Educational and Vocational History Questionnaire (Appendix 3.1). Are there any themes you can pick up that could help you to identify your skills and abilities? Psychologists tend to have strong skills in social interaction, verbal communication, understanding others, verbal reasoning, writing, scientific ability, problem solving, and statistics. If you have identified strengths in these areas, you might want to look a little closer at a major in psychology. Remember, however, that there are many other skills that could be helpful to psychologists (e.g., persuasiveness, mediation, mentoring, negotiating). Also, undergraduate psychology majors exhibit a wide range of transferable skills suitable for many professions, not just psychology.

There is a difference between your *self-estimated abilities*, or what you think you are good at, and what you are actually good at. There may be tasks that you do not think you are good at but that you actually could be good at with experience and practice. So, don't sell yourself short. For example, you might not think you are good in statistics, but it might just be that you have not had positive learning experiences in a supportive environment that encouraged these skills. Later in this chapter there is a section on self-efficacy that will help to get you thinking about your confidence in various areas. You also can learn more about your skills and abilities by completing a formal assessment of your abilities. Some career counselors use these assessments to help people gain an overview of their strengths and weaknesses.

VALUES

What is really important to you? Values can be extreme motivators. They represent principles, standards, or qualities that are inherently worthwhile or desirable to us. They can motivate us to behave in certain ways because of their intrinsic worth. Values, which are shaped by the cultural context of the individual and his or her life experiences, can give one's life and work meaning. If we believe in something strongly enough, or are passionate enough about something, we are likely to be highly motivated to behave in ways that are consistent with that value. Hence, individuals frequently experience values as standards that guide how they "should" behave (Brown, 2002). For example, if we strongly value helping others, we may be motivated to enter one of the helping professions.

For work to be meaningful and satisfying, it generally must be consistent with a person's value system. So, it makes sense that people tend to seek out jobs and careers that are consistent with their values and allow them to be their true selves. This partially explains why some people are unhappy with their occupational choices, even when they perform the tasks associated with those jobs in an exemplary manner (Brown, 2002).

One can never compile a complete list of values, but checklists can help you to initiate your self-exploration in this area. Try completing the values checklist in Appendix 3.3 and ranking your values in order of importance. How well do the values you ranked the highest match the careers and majors you are considering? What implications and conclusions might you draw based on the degree of correspondence that you discover? Also, what can you learn about your values from your responses on the Educational and Vocational History Questionnaire in Appendix 3.1?

Many psychologists value helping others, working with others, making a difference, respect, creativity, equality and inclusiveness among many other things. Psychologists and psychology majors are not a homogeneous group. So, if your values somewhat mirror these, they may be consistent with psychology and the helping professions.

SELF-EFFICACY

Self-efficacy refers to how confident you feel engaging in various activities (Bandura, 1986, 1997). How negatively or positively you view your abilities can affect your academic and career choices. If you have low self-efficacy in a particular area, you might have thoughts that will interfere with your ability to perform the task well and may feel discouraged or overwhelmed (Sharf, 2006). How self-efficacious or confident you feel is related to your expectations about how successful you will be; your interests, goals, choices, actions; and your actual performance (Lent, Brown, & Hackett, 1994).

One way to assess your self-efficacy is to assess your perceptions of your ability to perform activities successfully. Using the Self-Efficacy Questionnaire (Lenox & Subich, 1994b) in Appendix 3.4, try rating the degree to which you feel you can complete successfully each given task. After completing the inventory, think about the degree to which your self-efficacy across Holland's types matches your self-perceived interests in the same areas. For more information about the development and use of this measure, refer to Lenox and Subich (1994a).

If you find that both your interests and your self-perceived abilities are high on a particular type, you might want to find out more about college majors and careers that are similar to that type. If you find that your self-perceived abilities are low in areas of high interest, you may want to consider taking a class to develop your skills in that area. If your interests are low in areas of high self-perceived abilities, it may be either that you feel confident because you routinely perform those tasks but do not have a desire to pursue a career in that area or that you lack sufficient experience in that area to have well-developed interests in it. If this is the case, you might want to try engaging in tasks consistent with that type to gain more experience and perhaps refine your interests.

Similar to the RIASEC types discussed in the section on personality, psychologists tend to feel more self-efficacious in SIA tasks. An individual's experiences can either support a person's choice or be a barrier to obtaining a desired outcome, such as a career outcome. Barriers can include things like limited financial resources and discrimination, whereas supports include social support and encouragement. Both supports and barriers can affect self-efficacy, which in turn impacts career choice goals and actions (Lent et al., 1994). For example, you might be considering psychology as a major but worry that you will not be skilled enough in statistics. Think about how much exposure you have had to statistics. What were your learning experiences like? Did you feel supported and encouraged in math or statistics courses you have taken? If you have not taken a statistics course, try enrolling in one! Be mindful of finding sources of support and encouragement for your involvement in this course. Many career counselors help people further explore and improve their self-efficacy. If you think this is an issue for you, consider seeking help.

FEEDFORWARD FIRST

Feedforward first is a process that was introduced as an alternative to feedback interviews (Kluger & Nir, 2006). Feedforward is based on the Appreciative Interview (for a review, see Bushe & Kassam, 2005). I suggest that you use this process, with a slight adaptation, to explore and assess whether you are on the right educational and career path.

1. Write a narrative or story about a time that you were at your best. This could be an event, project, or assignment at school or work during which you felt energized (full of life, in flow), even before the results of your actions became known.
2. Include the conditions, in yourself, others, and the organization (school or work) that allowed this story to happen.
3. What was the peak moment of this story? What emotions did you feel then (including your physiological reaction)?
4. To what degree do your plans for the immediate future take you closer to, or further away from, the conditions that allowed you to feel alive and to be at your best?
5. How can you use this story, and your reflections above, to move toward greater alignment between your deep interests and your plans?

Exploring the World of Work

You may think you know a lot about work already. After all, you have been observing people work, and perhaps have had a few jobs of your own along the way. However, just like anything else, you don't know how much you don't know until you start looking for information. What kind of information should you be looking for? Where should you look for it? How do you get started? Those are the kinds of questions that are addressed in this section. What follows is a list of resources (such as college and university career services centers, Internet sources, public libraries, and professional organizations) and strategies (networking, informational interviewing, job shadowing) for learning more about various occupations. First, have a look at Exhibit 3.2 for an outline of the types of occupational information that you are looking for.

COLLEGE AND UNIVERSITY CAREER SERVICES CENTERS

If you are currently a college student, probably the best way to get started is by visiting your college or university career center. Most career centers also have Web sites with a wealth of information. Do not wait until you get an appointment. Have a look now at your institution's career center Web site and the Web sites of some of the most exemplary university career center home pages that are listed at the end of this chapter. There is plenty of readily available information that can keep you busy for hours. Of course, that could be a problem in itself—information overload. The

---

EXHIBIT 3.2

Types of Occupational Information to Research

The nature of the work
Duties and tasks
Working conditions
Educational preparation and professional training
Licensure, certification, or other professional credentialing
Earnings
Job advancement
Job outlook
Salary and benefits

---

best way to approach career exploration and information management is to have a road map—an idea of where you are and where you are going. Knowing the landscape is important. That means knowing what kinds of information you are looking for and how to use the information once you have it. Some strategies for making a good match between yourself and the world of work are offered later in this chapter.

Let's start with the kinds of resources that career services centers have to offer. In addition to the career assessment and counseling services that are described in chapter 4 of this volume, career centers offer many other tremendous resources. Typically, they offer career workshops, job fairs, and internship and job listings. They also tend to have a number of career exploration resources and tools available including books, DVDs, and self-assessments, including computer and Internet-based assessment and information. They also routinely provide assistance with graduate school preparation, resume writing, and interviewing—including mock interviews. Many college career centers or academic counseling departments provide career exploration courses, earning 1 to 3 credit hours, to help you with the process of career exploration and decision making. Career centers also tend to have excellent alumni networks and employer contacts to facilitate information gathering and job hunting.

OTHER RESOURCES FOR CAREER SEARCHES

The Internet

The Internet provides a seemingly endless supply of informational resources. Your challenge with the Internet is to be sure that you are using reputable sources for information and job hunting. How do you know if you can trust a Web site to provide accurate information? Look for who sponsors the site (provides financial support) and the credentials (academic degrees) of the people responsible for its content. For example, if the Web site provides information about the work roles of psychologists, did a licensed psychologist provide the information on the site? Is there a psychologist to contact for further information? Are there links to professional organizations for psychologists? A good source of information about any profession is a Web site sponsored by that profession's national, state, or local organization. Accredited university departments of psychology also are good sources of information about educational programs. As with any information you obtain, consider the source. Check out some of the links suggested at the end of this chapter.

Public Libraries

Many public libraries across the United States are developing virtual as well as in-person career centers. These career centers often offer similar resources to those available in a college and university career center and are free and available to the public. Explore what your local public library has to offer or check out the library Web sites suggested at the end of this chapter.

Professional Organizations

Professional organizations are excellent sources of information. For organizations relevant to psychology and other helping professions, take a look at the Web sites listed at the end of the chapter.

Networking

Your best source of information about possible jobs might be people that you know. Talk. Talk to everyone—then talk to them again. Talk with your friends, family members, professors, coworkers, and other knowledgeable people in the field. Professors, in particular, can be a great source of information and advice. They can give you information about the psychology major and other related college majors, as well as their own personal experiences in the field. Professors also can be a great source of referrals to broaden your network. They often know professionals working in other settings, alumni from your program, and other individuals—both on-campus and off—who can provide further information and unique perspectives.

Informational Interviewing

Informational interviewing involves contacting individuals who are in jobs or fields of interest to you and interviewing them to find out more about their occupation and profession. It involves going directly to the source—talking to real people with real jobs. You also have to recognize that this is not a source of unbiased information. People will give you their personal subjective experiences. That is not to say that this information is not useful, particularly if you obtain it from several different sources.

Informational interviews provide a window into working life. They provide you with the opportunity to learn more about careers, particular jobs, and job sites. You also can get answers to specific questions that you might have. How do you find people to interview, and once you find them, how do you approach them? Network. Get the names of people in the field from professors, people you have worked with, family members, friends, neighbors, career centers, or local professional organizations. You can even use the phonebook or Internet. When you have a list of the people you would like to contact, start making calls and sending e-mails. Tell them who you are and that you are interested in learning more about their career and work experiences. Let them know that you have some questions that you would like to ask them and see if it might be possible to meet with them for 20 minutes—then stick to the 20-minute time frame you promised. Many people who enjoy their work are happy to talk about themselves and their work. Asking for only 20 minutes keeps the demand on their time reasonable. What if someone denies your request? See whether they are willing to answer just a few questions on the phone, and ask them to recommend one or two people who might be available to meet with you.

The close of any informational interview is another time to be sure to ask for the names of other people that you might contact. Ask the people you are interviewing whether you can use their name as someone who referred you to their contacts. This could mean the difference between getting the interview and not getting it. Be sure to follow up the interview with a personal note of thanks, and keep these interviewees in your contact list for the future. (You never know when this list might come in handy.) Finally, think about returning the favor someday by letting someone interview you to find out more about your work!

How can you make the most of your informational interviews? Preparation. Learn as much as you can about the field and about that person's place of employment. Avoid spending any of your precious time, and theirs, asking questions that you could have learned the answers to elsewhere (like the company Web site). Make a list of questions in advance. Think about what you want to know, particularly the intangible information that cannot be found in books and other resources. For example, what can they tell you about workplace stress, work and family navigation, and lifestyle? Bring a typed list of your questions to the interview, dress as if you were going to a job interview, arrive on time, and stick to

EXHIBIT 3.3

Sample Informational Interview Questions

Tell me about the most interesting, satisfying, and challenging aspects of your job.

What are the most unappealing or frustrating parts of your job?

What is it like to work here? Is it similar to other places that you have worked?

What kind of lifestyle can one expect in this line of work?

What is valued by this field and this organization?

What does the future look like in this field?

What advice would you give someone like me just starting out in this field?

What do you know now that you wish you had known when you were starting out?

Can you tell me a little about your career path and how you got to be where you are now?

What else do you think would be important for me to know about this line of work?

Can you refer me to others who might be willing to talk with me about their work?

your agreed-on topic and length of time. Remember, this is not a job interview in disguise; you are seeking information, opinions, and advice. To get started, have a look at the sample questions in Exhibit 3.3.

Job Shadowing

Job shadowing—following along in someone's footsteps for a day—is another way to learn about what type of career appeals to you. You will have the chance to observe and experience what a typical day in a particular job is like. It is one thing to have a person tell you about his or her job and quite another to actually see that person in action and experience their job firsthand. What should you look for that day? Observe everything you can about the environment and the people in it. What is the work space like? Is it a serious and structured environment or a more flexible and adaptable one? What are the explicit and implicit expectations? Do people work alone or in groups? How do they interact and relate to each other? What are their communication styles like? What do they seem to value? Ask yourself if this is the kind of environment in which you would like to work or if these are the types of people that you would like to work with.

Strategies for Successful Decision Making

Decisions are always made under some degree of uncertainty because you can never know for certain how things will turn out in the future and what the outcome of your decisions will be. Furthermore, discriminatory attitudes and behaviors add to the uncertainty for women and minorities (Brown, 2002). Nonetheless, it is useful to have a plan to work from.

The best decisions are often made after you have looked closely at your own interests and gotten a true picture of the world of work. Some students who commit too early to a college major without first thoroughly exploring their alternatives may find that they have a tendency to *foreclose on* (prematurely rule out) their options. Try assessing the degree to which you have this tendency and your level of commitment to a career choice by completing the Commitment to Career Choices Scale (CCCS; Blustein, Ellis, & Devenis, 1987) found in Appendix 3.5. A higher score on the Tendency to Foreclose Scale of the CCCS suggests a stronger tendency to make a decision before engaging in adequate exploration. A higher score on the Vocational Exploration and Commitment Scale of the CCCS suggests more progression toward committing to an educational or career choice. For more information about the development and use of this measure, refer to Blustein, Ellis, and Devenis (1989).

Once you have gathered sufficient information about yourself and the world of work, it is time to start narrowing the field. Begin to narrow down your options based on what you have learned. Which college majors provide the best match for your interests, personality, values, skills, and abilities? You might want to check out O*NET online (http://online.onetcenter.org/) to find occupations by keywords or O*NET descriptors such as knowledge, skills, abilities, work activities, interests, and work values.

Decision making is a skill. There also are various decision-making styles or strategies. How people collect, process, and apply information is their decision-making style. Some people are thoughtful and methodical in their approach to listing and evaluating their alternatives. These people might find it useful to make a list of the pros and cons of pursuing a degree in each of the majors they are considering. They might then rank order their list according to those pros and cons that are the most important, meaningful, or relevant to them. Not everyone takes such a methodical approach to decision making, however. Others are more spontaneous or intuitive in reaching a decision. They make the choice that feels right. Still

EXHIBIT 3.4

Bad Reasons to Choose a Major

My (mother, father, partner) wants me to.

It is a really popular major.

It is as good as any other major.

My sister [brother, friend] had that major.

others use their relationships as resources in the process, seeking advice, encouragement, and support. People using this style might talk to people who are important to them to get their perspective on what they think would make a good match with their interests and abilities.

Decision making ultimately requires applying your values to your available options. Most people do this by evaluating the possible outcomes of their decisions and eliminating the least desirable alternatives. Some people use a single style or strategy, whereas others use several strategies to reach a decision. You may find that you use different strategies for different types of decisions.

Setting clear and identifiable goals is helpful in the decision-making process. With well-defined goals, you can aim to make decisions that will bring you closer to your ultimate goal. Decisions, like goals, can be broken down into short-range and long-range decisions. The decisions you make now will influence the options and choices you will have later.

Summary

There are many bad reasons to choose a major (see Exhibit 3.4 for just a few), but there are also some very good reasons. I hope that after engaging in the extensive exploration recommended in this chapter you will have begun to see the value of a good match. Eventually, only you can make the choice of college major among your best available options. So, is psychology the right major for you? Only you know the answer to that. However, you do not have to make that decision in isolation. The process of decision making is not always easy. As you have learned, there are many factors to consider. Decision making is a skill that many individuals can improve. If you are having trouble deciding, take a look at chapter 4 for more insight on the process of committing to a decision.

Suggested Web Sites

- The Career Key. This Web site provides information and assistance with career changes, career planning, job skills, and choosing a college major or educational program. For a nominal fee, it also includes a career assessment measure that assesses your skills, abilities, values, and interests (using the six Holland personality types that are most often used by professional career counselors). In addition to learning about yourself, it provides you with information about jobs that match your personality. See http://www.careerkey.org

- Quintessential Careers. This Web site provides numerous career development resources including information about career books, transferable skills, informational interviewing, and job hunting tools. The links to two pages that may be of particular interest are also provided. See http://www.quintcareers.com/
  - Informational Interviewing: http://www.quintcareers.com/informational_interviewing.html
  - Transferable Skills: http://www.quintcareers.com/transferable_skills.html

- O*NET Skills Search. Skills Search is designed to help you use your skill set to identify occupations for exploration. You select a set of skills from six broad groups of skills to create your customized list, and a list of matching occupations is generated for you. See http://online.onetcenter.org/skills/

- O*NET Find Occupations. This Web site helps you to find occupations using keywords or O*NET descriptors (such as knowledge, skills, abilities, work activities, interests, and work values). See http://online.onetcenter.org/find/

- Career Interests Game. Using Holland's personality types, this is a game designed to help you match your interests and skills with similar careers. See http://career.missouri.edu/students/explore/thecareerinterestsgame.php

- Self-Directed Search (SDS). For a nominal fee, try taking the SDS to assess your Holland personality type: http://www.self-directed-search.com

- Myers–Briggs Type Indicator® (MBTI). The MBTI instrument measures personality preferences on four different scales: Extraversion (E)–Introversion (I), Sensing (S)–Intuition (N), Thinking (T)–Feeling (F), and Judging (J)–Perceiving (P). Results from the indicator are a four-letter type. See http://www.capt.org/take-mbti-assessment/mbti.htm

- University of Wisconsin Stevens Point: Using the Internet for Career Exploration and Job Searches. This Web site provides how-to guides, search engines, and top suggested sites: http://www.uwsp.edu/career/InternetJobSearch.htm

▪ The Riley Guide. The Riley Guide is a directory of employment and career information sources and services on the Internet. It is primarily intended to provide instruction for job seekers on how to use the Internet to their best advantage. It lists many online sites and services that are useful for your job search. See http://www.rileyguide.com/

▪ The Riley Guide: Research & Target Employers and Locations. This Web site provides assistance in using the Internet for research to support your job search. It includes tips for doing online research, as well as information about how to find employers you may want to consider. See http://www.rileyguide.com/jsresearch.html

▪ Exemplary Public Library Career Centers. The following public library Web sites have extensive career information available online.
  ▪ Chicago Public Library: http://www.chipublib.org/008subject/002business/career.html
  ▪ Cuyahoga County Ohio Public Library: http://www.cuyahogalibrary.org/StdBackPage.aspx?id=1511

▪ Exemplary University Career Center Home Pages. The following college and university career development Web sites provide a wealth of information about college majors and career exploration tools.
  ▪ Arizona State University Career Services: www.asu.edu/career/
  ▪ Cleveland State University: http://www.csuohio.edu/career/
  ▪ Pennsylvania State University: http://www.sa.psu.edu/career
  ▪ University of Missouri–Columbia: http://career.missouri.edu
  ▪ University of Washington: http://depts.washington.edu/careers/students/
  ▪ Union College: http://www.union.edu/Career/index.php
  ▪ University at Albany, State University of New York: http://www.albany.edu/cdc/

Suggested Reading

Blocher, D. H., Heppner, M., & Johnston, J. (2001). *Career planning for the 21st century* (2nd ed.). Denver, CO: Love.

Bolles, R. N. (1998). *The what color is your parachute workbook.* Berkeley, CA: Ten Speed Press.

Bolles, R. N. (2005). *What color is your parachute?* Berkeley, CA: Ten Speed Press.

Appendix 3.1:
Educational and Vocational
History Questionnaire

Instructions: Provide complete and honest responses to each of the questions below. Completing an educaitonal and vocational history can provide valuable information to you that will assist you in making satisfactory educational and career decisions.

1. What are your conceptions of work? In other words, what are your attitudes, beliefs, and feelings about work?

2. What role does or will work play in your life?

3. Describe your school experiences (positive, negative, neutral).

4. List your five main fears about work or a career:

   1.

   2.

   3.

   4.

   5.

5. What are the three best educational or career decisions you have made?

   1.

   2.

   3.

6. What are the three worst educational or career decisions you have made?

    1.

    2.

    3.

7. Describe your early educational and career ambitions.

8. Describe your current educational and career ambitions.

9. How do your early and current educational and career ambitions compare?

10. Describe any obstacles, barriers, or roadblocks you have encountered or anticipate encountering (in yourself, others, or the world).

11. What implicit messages have you received about gender, race/ethnicity, and privilege?

12. Describe any educational or career failures you have experienced.

13. Describe any educational or career successes you have experienced.

14. List the people who have had the most influence on your career development:

1.

2.

3.

4.

5.

6.

7.

8.

9.

10.

15. Rank order the people you listed in Question 14. Describe how your relationships with the top two people on your list were influential in your career development.

1.

2.

16. Father's current occupation:

Brief history of father's work:

Briefly describe your father's feelings about his work:

What messages did you receive from your father about work?

17. Mother's current occupation:

Brief history of mother's work:

Briefly describe your mother's feelings about her work:

What messages did you receive from your mother about work?

18. Describe any other relevant information that would assist you in understanding your situation.

Appendix 3.2:
Self-Assessment of Skills and Abilities

Instructions: Place a check mark indicating your self-estimated level of abilities.

	Level of competence				
	Low		Average		High
Skills and abilities	1	2	3	4	5
Verbal reasoning					
Spatial perception					
Writing					
Verbal communication					
Social skills					
Persuasiveness					
Scientific ability					
Artistic ability					
Entrepreneurial skills					
Organizational skills					
Teaching ability					
Math ability					
Understanding others					
Managerial skills					
Mediation					
Mentoring					
Negotiating					
Public speaking					

Level of competence

Skills and abilities	Low		Average		High
	1	2	3	4	5
Presentation					
Team building					
Problem solving					
Budgeting					
Financial planning					
Marketing					
Mechanical ability					
Computer					
Advising					
Evaluating					
Statistical					
Auditing					
Coaching					
Judging					
Leading					
Motivating					
Planning					
Programming					
Reading					
Reasoning					
Scheduling					
Supervising					

Appendix 3.3:
Values Checklist

Instructions: Circle the values that are most important to you. Add other values not listed.

Family	Health	Freedom
Adventure	Creativity	Productivity
Spirituality	High income	Helping others
Social status and prestige	Influencing others	Flexible schedule
Authority	Competition	Working alone
Working with others	Leisure time	Responsibility
Travel	Meaningful work	Intellectual
Stimulation	Leadership	Challenge
Respect	Fame	Power
Making a difference	Recognition	Job security
Variety	Equality and inclusiveness	Competency
Achievement	Advancement	Autonomy
Work-life balance	Belonging to a group	Relationships
Integrity	Lifelong learning	Leisure
Personal growth	Risk-taking	Self-expression
Stability	_____	_____

Now identify your top ten values and rank order them below.

1.	4.	7.	10.
2.	5.	8.	
3.	6.	9.	

It is helpful to consider how well your values relate to your career choice. How well does the list of values you circled correspond with the careers you are considering?

Appendix 3.4:
Self-Efficacy Questionnaire

Instructions: Read each of the statements carefully. Mark next to each question the degree (1 to 10) to which you believe you have the abilities to complete the activities stated. A response of "1" indicates that you are completely *unsure* of your abilities to complete the activities. A response of "10" indicates that you are completely *sure* of your abilities to complete the activities. When answering, *do not* take into account whether you have actually performed the activity in the past or have been trained to perform the activity.

1	2	3	4	5	6	7	8	9	10
Completely unsure								Completely sure	

_____ 1. Indicate on the scale your degree of confidence in completing activities that require you to help people who are upset or troubled.

_____ 2. Indicate your degree of confidence in completing activities that require you to use algebra to solve mathematical problems.

_____ 3. Indicate your degree of confidence in completing activities that require you to keep accurate records of payments or sales.

_____ 4. Indicate your degree of confidence in completing activities that require you to write stories or poetry.

_____ 5. Indicate your degree of confidence in completing activities that require you to operate power tools such as a drill press or grinder or sewing machine.

_____ 6. Indicate your degree of confidence in completing activities that require you to take shorthand.

_____ 7. Indicate your degree of confidence in completing activities that require you to perform a scientific experiment or survey.

_____ 8. Indicate your degree of confidence in completing activities that require you to explain things to others.

_____ 9. Indicate your degree of confidence in completing activities that require you to get people to do things your way.

_____ 10. Indicate your degree of confidence in completing activities that require you to interpret simple chemical formulae.

_____ 11. Indicate your degree of confidence in completing activities that require you to use logarithmic tables.

_____ 12. Indicate your degree of confidence in completing activities that require you to arrange or compose music.

1	2	3	4	5	6	7	8	9	10
Completely unsure									Completely sure

_____ 13. Indicate your degree of confidence in completing activities that require you to make simple electrical repairs.

_____ 14. Indicate your degree of confidence in completing activities that require you to design clothing, posters, or furniture.

_____ 15. Indicate your degree of confidence in completing activities that require you to write news stories or technical reports.

_____ 16. Indicate your degree of confidence in completing activities that require you to change a car's oil or tire.

_____ 17. Indicate your degree of confidence in completing activities that require you to talk with all kinds of people.

_____ 18. Indicate your degree of confidence in completing activities that require you to participate in charity or benefit drives.

_____ 19. Indicate your degree of confidence in completing activities that require you to manage a sales campaign.

_____ 20. Indicate your degree of confidence in completing activities that require you to program a computer to study a scientific problem.

_____ 21. Indicate your degree of confidence in completing activities that require you to manage a small business or service.

_____ 22. Indicate your degree of confidence in completing activities that require you to be a good public speaker.

_____ 23. Indicate your degree of confidence in completing activities that require you to do a lot of paper work in a short time.

_____ 24. Indicate your degree of confidence in completing activities that require you to be a successful leader.

_____ 25. Indicate your degree of confidence in completing activities that require you to type 40 words a minute.

_____ 26. Indicate your degree of confidence in completing activities that require you to refinish furniture or woodwork.

_____ 27. Indicate your degree of confidence in completing activities that require you to plan entertainment for a party.

_____ 28. Indicate your degree of confidence in completing activities that require you to post credits and debits.

_____ 29. Indicate your degree of confidence in completing activities that require you to make simple plumbing repairs.

_____ 30. Indicate your degree of confidence in completing activities that require you to sketch people so that they can be recognized.

Scoring: Scores on each scale range from 5–50. Higher scores on each scale indicate a higher level of self-efficacy in that Holland type. Find your three highest scores and determine your Holland code for your self-perception of abilities.

Self-perceptions of **Realistic** Occupational Abilities: Add your scores on items 5, 13, 16, 26, 29.

Self-perceptions of **Investigative** Occupational Abilities: Add your scores on items 2, 7, 10, 11, 20.

Self-perceptions of **Artistic** Occupational Abilities: Add your scores on items 4, 12, 14, 15, 30.

Self-perceptions of **Social** Occupational Abilities: Add your scores on items 1, 8, 17, 18, 27.

Self-perceptions of **Enterprising** Occupational Abilities: Add your scores on items 9, 19, 21, 22, 24.

Self-perceptions of **Conventional** Occupational Abilities: Add your scores on items 3, 6, 23, 25, 28.

Note. From *Self-Efficacy Questionnaire*, by R. A. Lenox and L. M. Subich, 1994, unpublished manuscript. Copyright 1994 by the authors. Used with permission of the authors. All rights reserved.

Appendix 3.5:
Commitment to Career
Choices Scale

Instructions. In the items that follow, please indicate the appropriate number using the scale below that most accurately reflects the extent to which you agree or disagree with the statement. If you do not currently have a specific career goal, respond to the following items in a way that would reflect your behavior and attitudes if you did have an occupational preference. Place the appropriate number next to the item in the space provided.

1	2	3	4	5	6	7
Never true about me	Almost never true about me	Usually not true about me	No opinion/ not sure	Usually true about me	Almost always true about me	Always true about me

_____ 1. I believe that a sign of maturity is deciding on a single career goal and sticking to it.

_____ 2. Based on what I know about my interests, I believe that I am suited for only one specific occupation.

_____ 3. The chances are excellent that I will actually end up doing the kind of work that I most want to do.

_____ 4. I may need to learn more about myself (i.e., my interests, abilities, values, etc.) before making a commitment to a specific occupation.

_____ 5. It is hard for me to decide on a career goal because it seems that there are too many possibilities.

_____ 6. I have a good deal of information about the occupational fields that are most interesting to me.

_____ 7. I have thought about how to get around the obstacles that may exist in the occupational field that I am considering.

_____ 8. I think that a wavering or indecisive approach to educational and career choices is a sign of weakness; one should take a stand and follow through with it no matter what.

_____ 9. I believe that no matter what others might think, my educational and career decisions will either be right or wrong.

_____ 10. Based on what I know about my abilities and talents, I believe that only one specific occupation is right for me.

1	2	3	4	5	6	7
Never true about me	Almost never true about me	Usually not true about me	No opinion/ not sure	Usually true about me	Almost always true about me	Always true about me

_____ 11. While I am aware of my educational and career options, I do not feel comfortable committing myself to a specific occupation.

_____ 12. I feel uneasy about committing myself to a specific occupation because I am not aware of alternative options in related fields.

_____ 13. I find myself changing academic majors often because I cannot focus on one specific career goal.

_____ 14. I do not know enough about myself (i.e., my interests, abilities, and values) to make a commitment to a specific occupation.

_____ 15. I like the openness of considering various possibilities before committing myself to a specific occupation.

_____ 16. Based on what I know about the world of work (i.e., the nature of various occupations), I do not believe that I should seriously consider more than a single career goal at a time.

_____ 17. It is hard to commit myself to a specific career goal because I am unsure about what the future holds for me.

_____ 18. I find it difficult to commit myself to important life decisions.

_____ 19. I feel uneasy in committing myself to a career goal because I do not have as much information about the fields that I am considering as I probably should.

_____ 20. I have difficulty making decisions when faced with a variety of options.

_____ 21. I feel confident in my ability to achieve my career goals.

_____ 22. Based on what I know about my values (e.g., the importance of money, job security, etc.), I believe that only one single occupation is right for me.

_____ 23. I feel uneasy in committing myself to a specific career plan.

_____ 24. I think that I know enough about the occupations that I am considering to be able to commit myself firmly to a specific career goal.

_____ 25. I worry about my ability to make effective educational and career decisions.

_____ 26. I am not very certain about the kind of work I would like to do.

_____ 27. I would change my career plans if the field I am considering became more competitive and less accessible due to a decline in available openings.

_____ 28. I believe that there is only one specific career goal that is right for me.

Scoring: Please note that six of the items are reversed scored. The reversed scored items are as follows: 3, 6, 7, 15, 21, 24.

This means that you first have to reverse the score before you add it into the total. For example, if you responded with a 6 on Item 3, you need to perform a simple subtraction to reverse the score, $8 - 6 = 2$. Therefore, your score on item 3 is a 2. Reverse score each of the above items before you add them into the totals below.

Add your scores on the 9 items that make up the Tendency to Foreclose Scale, which are as follows: 1, 2, 8, 9, 10, 15, 16, 22, 28

Note. From *Commitment to Career Choices Scale*, by D. L. Blustein, M. V. Ellis, and L. E. Devenis, 1987, unpublished manuscript. Copyright 1987 by the authors. Used with permission of the authors. All rights reserved.

What if I Need Help Deciding? 4

S till can't decide? Although some people make decisions with apparent ease, many individuals face difficulties in making their career decisions. Why is this? What can you do about it if you are one of those people? This chapter provides answers to these and other questions about where to turn if you need help deciding on a college major. Vocational psychology researchers have been studying career indecision for many years. In writing this chapter, I relied on years of research and practice in understanding and assisting people who need a little extra help making educational and career choices.

Career Indecision

The clever title of a popular book published in the 1970s sums it up: *If You Don't Know Where You're Going, You'll Probably End up Somewhere Else* (Campbell, 1974). The opening words of the book are even more telling, "Unless you know what you want from life, you are not likely to stumble across it" (p. 7). Some people who are uncertain or undecided about what to do with their life choose to do nothing. What people often do not realize, however, is that doing nothing *is* doing something. Doing nothing puts you in the back seat and allows fate to take its course. There are chance events that occur and opportunities we never dreamed of that sometimes arise, but we can do things to prepare ourselves to be in a better position to take advantage of those chance events when and if they do occur. So, choosing to do nothing can severely limit your future opportunities and options. Even if you are unsure about what you want to do in the long run, doing something in the short run can ensure that you will have more choices in the future.

In the midst of trying to decide on a college major, you may reach a point of feeling stuck, not knowing what to do next. Perhaps you have conscientiously been reading this book and gathering information about yourself, the psychology major, and future opportunities but still cannot quite commit to a decision. As you progress through your undergraduate education, this might become a source of concern for you. Chapter 5 provides you with some strategies to manage the stress that often accompanies important decisions like deciding on a college major. In this chapter, however, you will learn more about how to move from a position of undecided to a committed stance with regard to your college major.

Feeling stuck might be accompanied by a number of thoughts and dilemmas. You might be confused or uncertain, have determined that the possibilities you were once considering no longer interest you, fear that you do not have what it takes for graduate study in psychology, or are overwhelmed by the diversity of paths one can take with an undergraduate degree in psychology. The best place to start if you have found yourself in this position is to find out why you are having difficulty. Discovering the sources of your decision-making difficulties is the first step in overcoming them.

Vocational researchers and theorists have developed a number of *taxonomies*, or categorical systems, to identify particular decision-making difficulties. One of the more widely known taxonomies was proposed by Gati, Krausz, and Osipow (1996). It is based on three levels of categorization. The first distinction is between difficulties arising before actually beginning the career decision-making process and those that arise during the process. The former set of difficulties involves a lack of readiness to enter the career decision-making process; the latter involves a lack of information and inability to make use of available information because it is inconsistent. Each of these three major categories of difficulties (lack of readiness, lack of information, and inconsistent information) is further divided into specific difficulty categories, for a total of 10 difficulty categories. These categories are depicted in Table 4.1.

To help locate the foci of difficulties, Gati et al. (1996) developed the Career Decision-Making Difficulties Questionnaire (CDDQ) based on the taxonomy described above. The CDDQ can be used as a diagnostic tool to help you locate difficulties that you may be facing in your decision-making process. It also can be used as an initial screening to help a career

TABLE 4.1

Categories of Difficulties on the Career Decision-Making Difficulties Questionnaire

Difficulty	Interpretation of high score
Difficulties arising prior to beginning the career decision-making process	
Lack of motivation	Reflects a lack of willingness to make a decision at this point in time.
General indecisiveness	Reflects a state of general difficulty in making decisions.
Dysfunctional beliefs	Reflects a distorted perception of the career decision-making process, as well as irrational beliefs and expectations about career decisions.
Difficulties arising during the career decision-making process	
Lack of information about the decision-making process	Reflects a lack of knowledge about how to reach a decision wisely and specifically about the steps involved in the career decision-making process.
Lack of information about the self	Reflects a situation where you feel that you do not have enough information about yourself.
Lack of information about occupations	Reflects a lack of information about existing career options: what alternatives exist and/or what each alternative is like.
Lack of information about additional sources of information	Reflects a lack of information about ways of obtaining additional information or help that may facilitate decision making.
Unreliable information	Indicates that you feel that the information you have about yourself or about the considered occupations contains contradictions.
Internal conflicts	Reflects a state of internal confusion. Such conflict may stem from difficulties in compromising between the many factors you view as important or from when some of these factors are incompatible with each other.
External conflicts	May indicate a gap between your preferences and the preferences voiced by significant others or between the opinions of two significant others.

Note. From *A Taxonomy of Career Decision-Making Difficulties*, 2001–2006, retrieved August 17, 2006, from http://kivunim.huji.ac.il/cddq/theory.htm. Copyright 2001–2006 by YISSUM. Adapted with permission.

counselor guide you in the counseling process. You can take this questionnaire online at http://www.cddq.org. The CDDQ takes approximately 7 to 12 minutes to complete and consists of 34 statements, each corresponding to a particular difficulty in the taxonomy just described. When completing the measure, you will be asked to rate each item on a 9-point scale according to how it best describes you (1 = *Does not describe me* to 9 = *Describes me well*). A score is generated in each of the 10 categories as outlined in Table 4.1. Once you complete the questionnaire, you immediately receive a summary of your results, including explanations of the various difficulties, and recommendations about how to overcome the difficulties. If the focus of your difficulties relates to lack of readiness to engage in the decision process, or emotionally related difficulties, it will be recommended that you receive assistance from a professional career counselor (as will be elaborated later in this chapter). If your difficulties focus on obtaining and using information needed for the decision, it will be recommended that you first review the three-stage systematic model for career decision making provided in the Web site.

The Three-Stage PIC model

The PIC model (P = prescreening, I = in-depth exploration, C = choice) was developed by Gati and Asher (2001) to help deliberating individuals make better and more systematic career decisions. This model is most helpful in decision situations (such as choosing a college major) in which you are faced with a fairly large number of educational, occupational, and career alternatives and need to take a large number of factors into account. Even if you already have a short list of optional college majors or occupations, you also may want to conduct a systematic decision process to make sure that your considered occupations are indeed those that best match your preferences and to stimulate new ideas for further consideration.

The uniqueness of the PIC model is that it offers you an opportunity to change the way you approach career decision making. When people face career decisions, usually they deal with them intuitively by comparing between occupations and choosing the most advantageous one. PIC offers to replace this perspective by focusing on career-related factors, instead of occupational titles. The term *career-related factors* (or *career-related attributes*) refers to all variables that can be used to characterize either individuals' preferences and abilities or career alternatives (e.g., income, length of training, physical work, mathematical skills). By choosing the career-related factors most important to you and using them to eliminate occupations that do not match your preferences, you will be able to learn more about your preferences regarding different occupational characteristics. For example, have you ever considered your willingness to work by yourself or in a group or your need for a varied versus a routine job? You might even come up with new ideas for occupations that you had not thought of before.

The goal of the first stage of the PIC model, the prescreening stage, is to identify a small number of promising alternatives that are compatible with your preferences and worthy of further exploration. In this stage, alternatives incompatible with your preferences are discarded and promising alternatives are retained. The purpose of the second stage of the PIC decision-making model, the in-depth exploration stage, is to gather extensive information about the promising alternatives. In this stage, you are encouraged to collect additional information about each of the alternatives to determine the degree to which each one matches your preferences. The goal of the third stage of the PIC model, the choice stage, is to choose the occupation that is most suitable for you. This involves the further processing of information gathered in the previous stage and making comparisons between the alternatives in order to locate the one that best matches your vision. The final step is to implement your decision. That means taking the necessary steps to make your choice become a reality.

To guide you through the three stages of the PIC model and to help you examine the compatibility between your preferences and occupations and locate promising career options and related occupational information, you may want to use an Internet-based interactive career decision-making system called Making Better Career Decisions (MBCD; Gati, 1996; Web site: http://mbcd.intocareers.org; note that the MBCD involves a nominal cost). The MBCD guides you through a step-by-step systematic career decision-making process based on the PIC model that takes approximately 30 to 60 minutes. First, you will be asked to identify and rank in importance the career factors or attributes (such as income level, independence, and the amount of travel required) that are most important to you. MBCD guides you to choose and rank 10 to 15 of the 28 attributes provided. You are then asked to mark the optimal (i.e., the most desirable) level of the most important attribute (e.g., mostly outdoors) and then to report which additional levels you regard as acceptable (e.g., only outdoors or an equal preference for indoors and outdoors). The purpose of providing the acceptable levels is to enable you to consider your willingness to compromise and to allow you to consider a broader range of possibilities. Both of these ratings are completed on a 5-point scale typically varying from *A great deal* to *Hardly ever.* Through a sequential elimination process, considering attribute after attribute (in the sequence of your importance ratings), alternatives that are not compatible with your preferences are eliminated until there is a small number of promising alternatives left. After completion of the prescreening stage described above, you receive a list of alternatives that were found to be compatible with your preferences—the "recommended list." Then, you can ask questions such as "Why not?"—why a particular option you were considering was not included in your recommended list. You also can revise your preferences on a given attribute and/or examine the compatibility between your preferences and a given occupation (e.g., psychology).

For carrying out the second stage of the PIC model—the in-depth exploration stage—MBCD offers comprehensive information regarding hundreds of occupational alternatives. You also can use the occupational information that you learned by following the suggestions provided for exploring the world of work in chapter 3. However, if you are continuing to struggle, you may not have adequately explored all of your available alternatives. Engaging in these exploratory tasks more thoroughly may prove to be useful—particularly if a lack of information was identified in the CDDQ as one of your major decision-making difficulties. A brief summary of the preferences that were used to locate the recommended occupations is also provided. You also can get a printed summary that can be a springboard for discussion and further exploration.

Comparing Your Intuitions With the Outcomes of Your Systematic Search

The systematic process of career decision making does not contradict the importance of *intuition* (a hunch or feeling about a particular career decision). Appropriate career decisions can be made actively, systematically, and consciously, yet intuition does have an important role to play in evaluating your final decision. This is important because not all people naturally approach decision making using a rational step-by-step procedure. Some people feel more comfortable using an intuitive approach—that is, doing what feels right. Similarities between the outcomes of the systematic decision process and occupational alternatives you find intuitively appealing can strengthen your confidence in your choice. If you come to a different decision using these two decision-making methods (systematic vs. intuitive), you may want to reexamine the decision-making process, locate the reason(s) for the incompatibilities, reconcile the differences, and arrive at a confident decision.

Positive Uncertainty

An alternative decision-making model is one proposed by Gelatt (1989), called *positive uncertainty.* Positive uncertainty is not the type of model that has a series of defined decision-making steps. Instead, it is a strategy or an attitude toward approaching decision making in an environment that is often unpredictable and uncertain. As such, this model suggests that "the best final decision may actually be a definite maybe" (Gelatt, 1989, pp. 255–256). Learning to keep an open mind and being able to change your mind when necessary or advantageous are skills that can serve a lifetime of decision making. Have a look at Exhibit 4.1 for a list of paradoxical principles developed by Gelatt (1991). These will be useful to keep in mind when decision making gets tough. It will become clear from reading these paradoxical principles that Gelatt's (1989, 1991) view of decision making emphasizes imagination, creativity, and intuition.

Constructivist Perspective

An alternative way to conceive of decision-making difficulties is from a *constructivist perspective.* That means that you come to understand your career indecision within the broader contexts of your life (e.g., work, family, relationships). The narrative method (Collin & Young, 1992) is one tool that encourages individuals to tell their life story as it pertains to their career decision-making difficulties (Stead & Watson, 2006). In telling one's story, one describes contextual factors that are meaningful to one's career decision-making problems. For example, an individual might describe difficulties choosing a college major within the context of negotiating a new set of family relationships in her newly blended family while at the same time facing financial difficulties. This individual may also be faced with the dilemma of choosing between her life dreams and interests and the college major that her parents would like her to choose.

Relational Perspective

In previous research (Schultheiss, 2003), I provided a framework for "relational career assessment" as a means of gaining additional insight into

EXHIBIT 4.1

Paradoxical Principles of Positive Uncertainty

1. Be focused and flexible about what you want.
   a. Know what you want but don't be sure.
   b. Treat goals as hypotheses.
   c. Balance achieving goals with discovering them.
2. Be aware and wary about what you know.
   a. Recognize that knowledge is power and ignorance is bliss.
   b. Treat memory as an enemy.
   c. Balance using information with imagination.
3. Be objective and optimistic about what you believe.
   a. Notice that reality is in the eye and the I of the beholder.
   b. Treat beliefs as prophecy.
   c. Balance reality testing with wishful-thinking.
4. Be practical and magical about what you do.
   a. Learn to plan and plan to learn.
   b. Treat intuition as real.
   c. Balance responding to change with causing change.

Note. From *Creative Decision-Making: Using Positive Uncertainty* (p. 12), by H. B. Gelatt, 1991, Los Altos, CA: Crisp. Copyright 1991 by Crisp. Adapted with permission of Axzo Press.

how relationships can influence decision making. This framework assumes that what transpires in our relationships can help or hinder our ability to effectively perform challenging career-related tasks such as choosing a college major. Relational career assessment begins with having you think about how your relationships (e.g., with parents, siblings, and significant others) may have influenced or affected your career exploration and decision-making processes. For example, how have specific aspects or qualities of these relationships influenced your thinking in these areas, positively or negatively? For further self-exploration, call to mind a difficult career decision that you have made. What role, if any, did relationships play in this decision?

Through relational career assessment, a better understanding can be gained of how others have been involved in your decision making and the effects of this involvement. The process of revealing meaningful relational influences may assist you in understanding the relational context within which you are striving for self-knowledge and making important choices.

As you can see, there are different ways to approach your career indecision to gain a better understanding of why you are stuck. You will have to decide for yourself if a rational, linear, systematic approach to decision making—or a more flexible, intuitive, and adaptable process—best fits with your personal style.

Career Counseling and Career Assessment

If the foci of your decision-making difficulties relate to internal or external conflicts that require more personal assistance, or if you still feel stuck after accessing the information provided in this chapter, consider seeking out a career counselor. A career counselor is someone who provides a trusting confidential therapeutic relationship and support and guidance with school and work challenges, such as the exploration of educational and work options. Career counseling is a process in which a counselor or psychologist works collaboratively with you to help you to clarify, specify, implement, and adjust to education and work-related decisions (Amundson, Harris-Bowlsbey, & Niles, 2005). Although the focus of career counseling is on education, career, and work concerns, there also is an explicit recognition of how work intersects with other aspects of your life.

Career professionals work collaboratively with their clients to accomplish the following:

■ administer and interpret formal and informal assessments;
■ encourage experience-based exploratory activities (such as job shadowing and occupational information interviews);
■ provide opportunities for improving decision-making skills;
■ assist in the development of individualized career plans;
■ teach job search strategies and interview skills and assist in resume development;
■ help resolve interpersonal conflicts on the job;
■ assist in understanding the integration of work and other life roles;
■ provide support for persons experiencing job stress, job loss, and other career transitions; and
■ help people face and overcome barriers to their career goals (Amundson et al., 2005).

As this list shows, career counseling involves, among other things, an individualized process of gathering and integrating information about yourself and the world of work and making educational and career related choices. Career counselors have available to them a number of assessment tools to help you to gain additional information about yourself, including your interests, values, skills and abilities, confidence, personality, and preferences (e.g., work environment, rewards). These assessment instruments are professionally developed questionnaires that can help you to better understand yourself in relation to college majors and the world of work.

A common misconception about career assessment is that tests tell you which career path to choose. Career assessment instruments do not provide answers; they provide information—information that can in turn generate ideas and help you begin dialogues with counselors, psychologists, and people who are important to you. These assessments are meant to be used as a springboard for self-understanding and further exploration. They are not intended to be the final word on what you should or should not do with your life.

How Do I Find a Career Counselor?

There are a number of ways you can get access to career counseling services. High school guidance counselors are a good source for career guidance. A likely alternative if you are a current college student is your college or university's career counseling center. Most universities have such centers, which provide services free of charge for their students and sometimes for their alumni. Career counselors also are in independent practice and work on a fee-for-service basis. To locate a career counselor near you, look in the yellow pages of your local phone book or on the Internet or seek a referral from someone you know and trust.

The National Career Development Association (NCDA) is a professional organization whose mission is to promote the career development of all people over the life span. NCDA provides services to the public and professionals involved with or interested in career development. On their Web site (http://www.ncda.org), NCDA provides consumer guidelines for selecting a counselor as well as links to search for a career counselor by state by using listings of master career counselors (MCCs) and master career development professionals (MCDPs). MCCs hold master's or doctoral degrees in counseling or related fields and also possess related credentials such as being a licensed counselor or licensed psychologist. These professionals are carefully screened to ensure that their level of expertise meets six or more of the NCDA counseling competencies. MCDPs include career development facilitators, career technicians, resume writers, employment agency professionals, career coaches, career management professionals, and workforce development professionals. The degrees, licenses, and levels of supervision of these professionals vary.

Summary

Many people need help with decision making at some point in their career. Some people need more help than others, and people need different kinds of help for different kinds of problems and dilemmas. You have probably realized in reading this chapter that there is no one correct way to make a decision. People arrive at their best choice through various paths. Chapter 5 will help you to manage the stress that is often associated with decision-making difficulties.

Suggested Web Site

■ Career Decision-Making Difficulties Questionnaire (CDDQ). The aim of this site is to assist individuals in making better career decisions. It includes links to the CDDQ, Prescreening, In-Depth Exploration, and Choice (PIC), and Making Better Career Decisions (MBCD) assessments. The Web site is maintained by Itamar Gati, Samuel and Esther Melton Chair in Education, Departments of Education and Psychology, Hebrew University of Jerusalem, Jerusalem 91905 Israel. E-mail: itamar.gati@huji.ac.il. See http://www.cddq.org

Suggested Reading

Gelatt, H. B. (1991). *Creative decision making.* Los Altos, CA: Crisp.

Luzzo, D. A. (Ed.). (2000). *Career counseling of college students: An empirical guide to strategies that work.* Washington, DC: American Psychological Association.

Handling the Stress Associated With Important Life Decisions

In a world that has become more uncertain and unpredictable, decisions and transitions relevant to school and work present highly challenging and potentially anxiety-producing situations. The choice of a college major is only one decision-making event among many that you will experience throughout your education and work life. Career choice is a lifelong process that increasingly involves a process of coping with unpredictable changes and opportunities (Blustein, 2006; Bright & Pryor, 2005). Hence, how you handle the stress of choosing a college major can set the stage for how you handle the stress associated with other important life decisions in the future. Although choosing a college major may be stressful for some people, others may make this decision without any undue stress. Both are normal reactions. Whether you are a decision maker who experiences excessive stress or does not experience such stress, this chapter will provide you with successful strategies for turning challenges into opportunities. An important aspect of career planning and decision making involves learning to take care of yourself, developing active social support networks, and achieving a balanced lifestyle. Therefore, taking stock of your available coping strategies and relational resources now will serve you well in the future across a variety of life stressors. In this chapter, you will learn about the nature of stress and anxiety and successful management strategies.

Stress

Stress has been described as a perceived threat to any important or fundamental human need (Blocher, Heppner, & Johnston, 2001). It can be experienced both physically (e.g., headaches and stomachaches) and mentally (e.g., anxiety). Stress can be generated by both internal and external circumstances. For example, failing to achieve an important goal, such as choosing a major, can be experienced as a threat to a person's self-esteem and respect. Stress in one area of your life (such as choosing a major) can spill over to other areas of your life (such as personal and family relationships). Similarly, certain factors such as family expectations and perfectionist characteristics can exacerbate the stress of choosing a major. You may really want to major in psychology, but your parents may want you to pursue a major in engineering or information technology. The stress you experience from choosing a major may actually impede your progress toward this goal unless you develop and use effective stress-management strategies.

Remember that stress is not always harmful. At times, it can be a motivating factor for learning and growth. When we face a stressful situation or problem, we are afforded the opportunity to master the environment and gain a greater degree of control over our lives. Healthy development and career progress involve managing and regulating stress levels in ways that allow us to succeed and grow.

It is important to learn to deal with the factors that cause stress in our lives. Blocher et al. (2001) have identified five key factors that cause stress: novelty, intensity, ambiguity, complexity, and involvement. Novelty is the most common factor that leads to, or produces, stress. *Novelty* refers to new and therefore unfamiliar situations, such as beginning a new class, meeting new people, starting a new job, and beginning a new major. When we anticipate or fear negative outcomes, our stress and anxiety increases. We may fear that we will fail in a new class or job or be rejected by new people we meet. Without novelty, our lives would quickly become monotonous. Therefore, our goal is to learn to manage the stress associated with novelty. One way to do this is to relate the new or novel situation to other situations that we have encountered and mastered in the past or to rely on role models who have successfully managed novelty. We also can gain more information about the situation to minimize the unknown.

High-intensity stimuli, such as the intense expression of emotions, are stressful events. We each need to know our own tolerance for these events and avoid unreasonable levels of stress in this regard. For example, if discussions with your friends about your major and life after college cause you undue anxiety that interferes with your ability to concentrate and get back to your work, you may want to avoid these intense experiences in the future (particularly the night before a big test). *Ambiguity* refers to a lack of structure in a situation that makes it difficult or impossible to interpret expectations, choose among alternative actions, or predict outcomes. One way to cope with ambiguity is to try to reduce it. You also might try to adapt and learn to live with ambiguity. Being flexible, adaptable, and able to tolerate ambiguity are 21st-century skills. Dealing with complex situations also can create stress. Educational and career decisions are rarely simple. Instead, they are typically complex and require us to process a huge amount of information and weigh a large number of factors. Our level of involvement (including psychological involvement) in a situation can increase stress levels. The more actively and emotionally involved we are in the process of choosing a major, the more stress we may experience. One way to manage this type of stress is by trying to see value in many outcomes. This takes the pressure off and, as a result, lowers the level of stress that is experienced.

Anxiety: What It Is and How It Can Be a Problem

Anxiety is typically defined as a diffuse, vague, and unpleasant feeling combining fear, apprehension, and worry (Sarason & Sarason, 2002) and is often experienced as pervasive worry and intrusive thoughts about possible future events and outcomes. It includes feelings of uncertainty, helplessness, and physiological arousal (i.e., rapid heart rate, shortness of breath, diarrhea, loss of appetite, fainting, dizziness, sweating, sleeplessness, frequent urination, and tremors). Anxiety can be adaptive if the discomfort is motivating. Chronic and intense anxiety, on the other hand, can be maladaptive and can interfere with new learning and career exploration.

At least three different forms of career anxiety have been identified in college students: fear of failing in one's academic or professional career, fear that one's parents might be disappointed in one's career choice, and fear of moving away from family and intimate relationships as a consequence of job or academic requirements (Vignoli, Croity-Belz, Chapeland, de Fillipis, & Garcia, 2005).

Research has demonstrated consistently that anxiety is associated with career indecision (i.e., a normal developmental phase that is fairly easily resolved for most people) and indecisiveness (i.e., more pervasive, severe, and chronic difficulties in making career decisions; see, e.g., Fuqua, Seaworth, & Newman, 1987; Kaplan & Brown, 1987). On the basis of this research, Saka, Gati, and Kelly (2006) identified four categories of the effects of anxiety on specific aspects of the career decision-making process.

The first category, *anxiety about the process*, refers to feelings of stress and anxiety arising just prior to actually beginning the decision-making process or anxiety evoked by excessive perfectionism about the process. The second category, *anxiety related to the uncertainty involved in choosing*, refers to three facets of uncertainty: uncertainty about the future, anxiety about being in an undecided state, and anxiety related to low tolerance for ambiguity. The third category, *anxiety about choosing*, includes four characteristics: perfectionism about choosing (i.e., having to find the "perfect occupation"), fear of losing other potentially suitable options, fear of choosing an unsuitable (i.e., "wrong") occupation, and anxiety about one's responsibility for the choice (especially a wrong one). The fourth category, *anxiety about the outcomes,* refers to a situation in which the individual already has some alternatives in mind, but is unable to actualize them due to fear of failure or of not fulfilling one's expectations and preferences in the chosen occupation.

Anxiety and Career Myths

Some beliefs people hold about themselves and the world of work are appropriate and foster meaningful career development whereas others create anxiety and hinder career decision making. Common irrational beliefs or myths include the notion that you should be competent, adequate, and achieving in all that one does if you are to be considered worthy; that there are invariably right, perfect, and precise decisions; and finally, that it is catastrophic if the "correct" choice is not made (Ellis & Dryden, 1997). Career myths, also called *dysfunctional career beliefs*, can prevent you from seriously considering available options, thereby constricting the career choice process. Some examples of dysfunctional career beliefs include the belief that there is one perfect major, there is only one career in the world that is right, choosing a major is a one-time event, and choosing a major is equivalent to choosing the content area of your life's work. Such beliefs could be obstacles to effective career decision making in that they are grounded in faulty assumptions, selective information, and misinformation (Stead & Watson, 1993).

The Career Myths Scale (Stead, 1991), provided in Appendix 5.1, can be used to assess the dysfunctional career beliefs that you may hold during the career choice process. Your score on this measure might provide you with some insight into the career beliefs that you hold that may be unknowingly creating or exacerbating symptoms of anxiety. Higher scores represent more dysfunctional career beliefs. After identifying these mistaken beliefs, you can then dispute and replace them with more functional ones. This process might be helpful in enabling you to be less restrictive in considering college major and career choices (Schultheiss & Stead, 2004). For more information about the development and use of this measure, refer to Stead and Watson (1993).

Managing Stress and Anxiety

You may now be beginning to develop a clearer understanding of what anxiety is and how and why it might occur. You might even see aspects of yourself in some of the previous descriptions. You may still be wondering, however, "What can I do about it?" Together with a good appraisal of the stressful situation or event, one should also take stock of one's resources for coping with the stress. The resources that are most frequently relied upon include supportive relationships, self-care, relaxation strategies, structured routines, time management, and mindfulness practices.

SUPPORTIVE RELATIONSHIPS

It is important to identify people, such as family members, peers, co-workers, and supervisors, from whom you can derive support and comfort. Recent research suggests that interpersonal connection facilitates career progress (Blustein, Schultheiss, & Flum, 2004; Schultheiss, 2003). More specifically, relationships with significant people in our lives play an important role in our ability to successfully negotiate career development tasks such as choosing a major. In fact, research has suggested that relationships are most important in the career-development process at times when you are making career decisions, assessing or affirming educational and career commitments, and making educational and career transitions (Schultheiss, Palma, Predragovich, & Glasscock, 2002). Important people in our lives can be influential in a number of ways by serving as a confidante (having someone to talk things over with) or role model; providing emotional support, encouragement, belief in our abilities, tangible assistance, and information; and offering guidance and advice on how to handle difficult situations. Your social support network also could include people who have had similar life experiences. People who have been in our shoes can sometimes offer the wisdom and support we need.

Certainly there also are less helpful, and neutral, ways that people influence our career decisions and progress. For example, some people feel that others try to force them into doing something without considering their interests or desires, and some experience others' actions as negative and critical. Neutral types of involvement are when important people offer broad and general statements without much follow-through, such as, "Do whatever makes you happy."

The first step in deriving as much support as you can from your relationships is to identify how the significant people in your life are involved in your career decision making. Through a process of identifying your positive, facilitative relationships, as well as any neutral, negative, or conflict-inducing people in your life, you will gain a better perspective on how you can best rely on others to your advantage. This process was described in more detail in chapter 4 of this volume.

The next step is to work to become better equipped to draw effectively on relationships with others as resources in the career development process and to benefit from deepened and more meaningful connections with others. For example, try reaching out and connecting with others to discuss the important issues that emerge in your decision-making process. Ask for feedback and others' opinions. Nurturing healthy and productive interactions with others, including deriving support from important people in your life, can be affirming and enhance your self-worth and self-efficacy. Having someone who provides a safe and comforting space to be vulnerable and discuss your fears and concerns can be gratifying and growth enhancing.

When you identify shortcomings in your network of relationships, consider how you might improve your relationships by perhaps resolving a prolonged conflict, or alternatively, how you can expand your interpersonal circle to include others who offer meaningful connections. Knowing whom to involve and how to involve them is your first step in deriving support from others and obtaining relief from the stress and anxiety that can so often occur amidst challenging and stressful events. Turning to your relationships with significant people in your life might be particularly useful, not only when you are experiencing heightened anxiety but also when you have reached an impasse using the more traditional approaches to career exploration and decision making discussed in chapters 3 and 4 of this volume.

Building and nurturing an effective social support network is an important aspect of self-care. Therefore, it is important to put time and energy into developing and maintaining a supportive web of relationships.

SELF-CARE

Self-care refers to an awareness of your need to take responsibility for your own health and wellness. There is an increased recognition that health is not restricted to the physical part of our lives. Instead, compelling research suggests a mind and body connection. If one part of our life is out of balance, then the other parts are likely to be affected (Blocher et al., 2001). For example, our mental or emotional health is linked to our overall wellness. When people experience any of a number of negative emotions (e.g., depression, anger, and anxiety) and do not find appropriate outlets to express or work through these feelings (either through self-care or professional mental health care), their physical health can suffer.

Blocher et al. (2001), prominent counseling psychologists who have devoted their careers to assisting people with developmental transitions, have insisted that to make good career choices and to have the energy to conduct an effective career planning process, you must be healthy in body and mind. Blocher et al. asserted that you must keep yourself in optimal health through self-care activities to cope successfully with stressful situations such as choosing a college major or choosing among available career alternatives. It is important to develop an awareness of the patterns in your life that are health enhancing and those that are health defeating so that you might begin to change those patterns that may be detrimental to your health. Blocher et al. outline three major areas for self-care: physical, mental or emotional, and spiritual. Each of these will be discussed next.

Physical self-care involves such things as diet and exercise, which play important roles in physical and mental health. Both have been linked to many major diseases. For many people, their diet suffers when they are under stress or feeling anxious or depressed. Food is sometimes perceived as a source of comfort. Although comfort foods may temporarily take our minds off of our worries or relieve boredom, they are typically not healthy choices and work against improving our well-being. In addition to food, exercise is critical in strengthening one's body, reducing the chance of stress and disease, increasing mental acuity, increasing stamina, promoting better sleep, lessening depression, and promoting higher self-esteem. Try analyzing your diet and evaluating the amount of exercise that you get. If you start slowly with an exercise routine and give yourself positive reinforcement for small steps, exercise will soon become reinforcing in itself.

Feeling down, anxious, irritable, or discouraged can be normal reactions to stressful situations such as making an educational or work decision. These emotions become problematic when they are prolonged, intense, or out of proportion to the presumed stressor. They also become problematic when they lead us to engage in self-defeating, unproductive, or unhealthy behaviors. Therefore, it is important to monitor your feelings and thoughts so that they do not lead you into problems, which is what is meant by mental and emotional self-care. For example, you could identify self-defeating thoughts and irrational beliefs and replace them with self-affirming statements.

Spiritual self-care involves recognizing the importance of finding meaning in your life and feeling connected in a broader way to nature and the universe. Given that many people derive meaning from their work, changes in school and work can be disruptive. You might find yourself questioning who you are, where you are going, and what your purpose is in life. Finding meaning in your life can be a very personal journey that involves self-reflection and trusting your feelings and values. Self-care in this area means engaging in the sort of self-reflection that will assist you in clarifying and seeking out what you want most out of life and what you ultimately find most satisfying.

RELAXATION STRATEGIES

Any of a number of relaxation strategies may help minimize the effects of stress and anxiety. Some of these exercises include deep breathing, progressive muscle relaxation, and imagery. Taking deep, slow, long breaths works to counteract the body's automatic reaction to stress—which is to engage in rapid shallow breathing, thereby increasing your body's stress response. *Progressive muscle relaxation*, which involves alternatively tensing and relaxing your muscles from head to toe, is a good way to relieve muscle tension. The muscle tension that often accompanies stress can lead to headaches, stiff necks, and back pain. *Imagery* involves sitting in a comfortable and quiet place, closing your eyes, and imagining that you are in a peaceful and relaxing place such as at the ocean, in the mountains, by a lake, or watching a sunset. It is important that you imagine as many relevant sensory details as you can. Imagine what you would see, hear, smell, taste, and feel. Engage in deep breathing as you imagine your relaxing scene and feel the tension in your muscles melt away. Try playing soft music while you are relaxing and imagining this special place. Have a look at Table 5.1 for other relaxation strategies and at the recommended Web site links and books at the end of this chapter for additional information about these and other relaxation techniques.

STRUCTURED ROUTINES

Another way to cope with stressful situations is to embed oneself in a daily routine because structure and routine provide stability and security

TABLE 5.1

Effective Relaxation Strategies

Strategy	Examples
Take time out	Take a break from what you are doing. Try taking a walk, getting some fresh air, or phoning a friend.
Exercise	Aerobic exercise helps to aid relaxation.
Take a hot bath or shower	Warm water helps to relieve muscle tension.
Read a book	Find a quiet place and a favorite book.
Listen to music	Soft, soothing music can help you to unwind and relax.
Write in a journal	Writing can be a way to release your worries and concerns.
Create art	Engage in creative self-expression.
Laugh	Humor can be good therapy.
Socialize	Spend time with family and friends.
Rest	Be sure to get adequate sleep.

in everyday life. For example, try to maintain routine sleeping and eating schedules and typical social and recreational activities. When you allow a stressful situation to disrupt your regular routines, you are vulnerable to fixating and focusing solely on the stressful situation, making yourself even more vulnerable to anxiety and its ill effects. The routines of sleep, nutrition, exercise, and relaxation are key structured routines that facilitate healthy functioning.

TIME MANAGEMENT

Most people have the capacity to manage their time better. Good time management makes the working day more productive and leisure time more fulfilling. The sequence in which you perform daily tasks can have a profound effect on your productivity and relaxation. Manage your time and create a schedule that works for you. If you are most alert in the morning, set aside morning hours to study. If you study best late at night, have your day organized so that you can work at night. It also is important to schedule breaks, leisure activities, and other obligations and responsibilities. A well-balanced lifestyle will minimize stress, and benefit you in all areas of your life. Try these suggestions offered by Landrum and Davis (2004).

- Set aside a time and place to study.
- Set priorities, and do things in that order.
- Break down large projects into smaller tasks.
- Plan a reasonable number of tasks that you are likely to be able to accomplish in a day.
- Work on one important task at a time.

- Be specific in defining your tasks. For example, "write the outline for the paper," instead of "work on paper."
- Check your progress frequently.

Be realistic about what you can actually achieve in a day. Setting your expectations too high can leave you feeling chronically stressed and frustrated. If possible, find ways to cut back on your activities and responsibilities, either temporarily or permanently.

Goal setting and planning are essential skills in managing your time. Having clear short- and long-term goals is essential for prioritizing your use of time. Whether your long-term professional goals include graduate school or finding a job immediately after graduation, success will require that you break down your long-term plans into manageable monthly, weekly, and daily tasks. Refer to chapter 9 (this volume) for a basic timetable for preparing yourself for graduate school and to chapter 8 (this volume) for the basic tasks required for completing a successful job search.

MINDFULNESS PRACTICES

Recent articles and books (e.g., Germer, Siegel, & Fulton, 2005; Wallace & Shapiro, 2006) evidence a growing awareness and appreciation of Eastern mindfulness-based practices that contribute to greater mental health. *Mindful awareness*, which is mostly experiential and nonverbal (i.e., sensory, somatic, intuitive, and emotional; Germer et al., 2005), is an acquired skill that allows us to be less reactive to what is happening in the moment. This skill takes practice to develop. *Mindfulness* is nonjudgmental moment-by-moment awareness of present experience with acceptance, a willingness to let things be just as they are the moment we become aware of them and accepting both pleasurable and painful experiences as they arise (Germer, 2005). Setting aside thoughts of the past and future is believed to help us respond more skillfully to new situations and to contribute to a less reactive autonomic nervous system—leaving us feeling less stressed.

Mindfulness is a life-enriching opportunity for learning and growth. It is a way of relating to experience that lessens the discomfort of life's difficulties—especially those that are seemingly self-imposed (Germer, 2005). So, why take a mindfulness-based approach to warding off anxiety? Moment-to-moment awareness is thought to dismantle anxiety by distinguishing the "facts" of sensory experience from the frightening conclusions that we draw from them (Germer, 2005).

A typical mindfulness exercise might require that you bring yourself into the present experience by focusing on your posture, closing your eyes, and asking yourself, "What am I experiencing right now in bodily sensations, feelings, and thoughts?" Your attention might first be directed to your breathing to anchor you in the moment, then slowly be expanded to your sense of your body as a whole. For further information about mindfulness, and additional mindfulness exercises, consult the suggested reading listed at the end of the chapter.

COUNSELING

When self-care strategies do not seem to be doing the trick and you need a little bit more help, consider seeking counseling. Most colleges and universities have counseling centers where individual counseling is provided for free or for a reduced fee for current students. Personal and career counseling are intertwined. That is, new models of counseling take a holistic approach across life roles. Counselors who are knowledgeable about the role of work in people's lives are skilled at integrating work and nonwork issues into the counseling process. Experiencing anxiety, depression, or other emotional difficulties during periods of stress sometimes happens despite one's best preventive efforts. Getting the care you need is your first step toward facilitating your well-being and the well-being of those closest to you. If you are not currently a student or would rather seek services from a community practitioner, other resources are available for counseling. To find a licensed practitioner, consult your medical insurance, yellow pages (under psychologists, counselors, or social workers), family, friends, or physician, or consult a list of licensed practitioners through state licensing boards. The Web site of the Association of State and Provincial Psychology Boards links to all U.S. state and Canadian psychology licensing boards (http://www.asppb.org/about/boardContactStatic.aspx). Through this Web site you can link to your state's psychology board to find a licensed psychologist in your community. Similarly, the National Board for Certified Counselors provides a database of licensed counselors on their Web site (http://www.nbcc.org/counselorfind2), as does the National Association of Social Workers (http://www.helpstartshere.org/common/Search/Default.asp).

Summary

Choosing a college major may or may not be a stressful event for you. Whether it is or not, you will face countless educational and career decisions over your life and encounter other transitions and important life decisions that may present challenging and stressful situations. This chapter has provided you with the knowledge and tools you will need to identify and manage the stress that often accompanies the making of major life choices. It also is important to keep a good repertoire of self-care strategies at hand to promote and enhance wellness. When extra help is needed along the way, seek out the professional help of a counselor or other trained mental health professional.

Suggested Web Sites

- Navy Environmental Health Center: http://www-nehc.med.navy.mil/hp/stress/relaxation_strategies.htm
- University of Minnesota: University Counseling & Consulting Services: http://www.ucs.umn.edu/lasc/handouts/relaxstrat.html
- Western Washington University Counseling Center: http://www.wwu.edu/chw/counseling/specific_topics/stress_bio/stress_tips.html

Suggested Reading

Blocher, D. H., Heppner, M., & Johnston, J. (2001). *Career planning for the 21st century* (2nd ed.). Denver, CO: Love.

Csikszentmihalyi, M. (1991). *Flow: The psychology of optimal experience.* New York: HarperCollins.

Edworthy, A. (2000). *Managing stress.* Philadelphia: Open University Press.

Gunaratana, B. (2002). *Mindfulness in plain English.* Somerville, MA: Wisdom.

Harris, C. (2003). *Minimize stress, maximize success: Effective strategies for realizing your goals.* San Francisco: Chronicle Books.

Kabat-Zinn, J. (1994). *Wherever you go, there you are: Mindfulness meditation in everyday life.* New York: Hyperion.

Linden, W. (2005). *Stress management: From basic science to better practice.* Thousand Oaks, CA: Sage.

Appendix 5.1:
Career Myths Scale

Instructions: This questionnaire consists of statements that people commonly make regarding careers. Read through each item carefully and place the appropriate number next to the item in the space provided.

1	2	3	4	5
Strongly Disagree	Disagree	Uncertain	Agree	Strongly Agree

_____ 1. If I do <u>not</u> do well in the career of my choice I will lose my self-respect.

_____ 2. A test that measures which careers are suited to me will indicate the right career for me.

_____ 3. It would be a sign of weakness if I were uncertain about my choice of career.

_____ 4. The career I choose should satisfy the people who are important to me.

_____ 5. Psychological tests will tell me exactly which career I should enter.

_____ 6. If I make the right career choice I will succeed in that career.

_____ 7. I must know everything about a career before I decide to enter it.

_____ 8. A test that can tell me which careers I am interested in will indicate the best career for me.

_____ 9. A career must interest me a lot before I decide to enter it.

_____10. I shall only be happy when I find the career that satisfies all my needs.

_____ 11. My worth as a person will depend on my making the right career choice.

_____ 12. I will have a very low opinion of myself if I am not more successful than the people I shall work with.

_____ 13. Psychological tests will definitely help me to choose the career best suited to me.

_____ 14. If I carefully choose a career I will do very well in that career.

_____ 15. Psychological test scores will give me a strong indication of whether or not I will be successful in the career of my choice.

_____ 16. I will be extremely troubled if I am unsuccessful in the career of my choice.

_____ 17. If I select the right career I will become a happy person.

_____ 18. I must be strongly attracted to a career before I decide to enter it.

1		2	3	4	5
Strongly Disagree		Disagree	Uncertain	Agree	Strongly Agree

_____ 19. If I enter a high-status career, my future happiness will be assured.

_____ 20. A test that measures my academic ability will indicate the best career for me.

_____ 21. I would be very unhappy if the career I entered did not satisfy all my needs.

_____ 22. The opinion I have of myself will be determined largely by the career I choose.

_____ 23. A test that measures my abilities will indicate the best career for me.

_____ 24. It is essential that I make the right career choice as I will probably remain in that career for the rest of my life.

_____ 25. If I carefully plan my future career, I will not have any problems in reaching my career goals.

_____ 26. The only people who really know which career I should enter are career counselors.

_____ 27. If I carefully plan the career of my choice, I will be happy in that career.

Scoring: Add your total score from your responses above.

Note. From *The Career Myths Scale*, by G. B. Stead, 1991, unpublished manuscript, Vista University, Port Elizabeth, South Africa. Copyright 1991 by the author. Used with permission of the author. All rights reserved.

Getting the Most Out of My Major in Psychology

6

N ow that you have made the decision to major in psychology, do not put off getting the most out of your major until you are almost ready to graduate. Getting involved early in your college experience, and staying involved, is the secret to success. You know the old saying, "The early bird gets the worm"? Well, taking initiative early gets you noticed by faculty members and affords you the chance to be in the right place at the right time to take advantage of opportunities when they become available. By taking the initiative to get involved early, you also will be learning valuable skills and abilities that will benefit you throughout your career. Learning how to network, get yourself noticed, and gain beneficial learning experiences are all part of the covert curriculum that are too important to overlook.

This chapter provides you with strategies to gain a competitive edge in the job market and the graduate school application process. It includes tips on the importance of earning good grades, developing professional relationships with faculty, finding a mentor, engaging in research, seeking out field experiences, becoming involved in student and professional organizations, becoming active in extracurricular and volunteer activities, and broadening your horizons by learning about international psychology. Activities encouraging you to consider what you can do now (Exhibit 6.1) and what you can do next (Exhibit 6.2) will challenge you to begin your quest to get the most you can out of your college experience as a psychology major.

EXHIBIT 6.1

What Can I Do Now?

Talk to one instructor individually outside of class.

Visit your university's career development center.

Do an informational interview with a person in the field.

Check a book out of the library on careers in psychology and/or mental health.

Search the Internet for career resources in psychology.

Talk to a psychology major who is a graduating senior.

Shadow a psychologist or mental health professional.

Join a student organization or become a student member of a professional organization.

Earn Good Grades

Earning good grades is extremely important, especially if you have an interest in going to graduate school. Poor grades obtained while you are having fun the first year or two of college can be hard to overcome later. College-level coursework is different from high school–level work. Students in college are expected to be much more independent and accountable for what they learn. You may find that you need to develop new study skills or hone the skills you currently have. Most colleges and universities have a freshman course (sometimes called "Freshman Seminar" or "Freshman Experience") that teaches you the study skills that you will need to succeed in college. Do not be ashamed if you need extra help. Most universities have many resources available to assist students with learning difficulties. For example, many universities have writing centers to help students improve their writing skills so they can successfully complete literature reviews and research papers. College counseling centers frequently offer study skills workshops to help students study more effectively and efficiently. Other resources include joining or setting up a study group or checking out textbook Web sites for additional study tools. Have a close look at your course textbooks for information about the availability of a textbook companion Web site. Good note-taking and test-taking skills are crucial to obtaining good grades, so I offer some strategies next.

NOTE-TAKING SKILLS

Listening attentively to lectures can be difficult, but the effective student must be able to identify important points and take accurate notes. Im-

EXHIBIT 6.2

What Can I Do Next?

Prepare your resume.

Explore internship opportunities and choose one.

Explore faculty research interests and join a research team.

Explore graduate programs in psychology.

Explore career opportunities for psychology major graduates.

Explore career opportunities for psychology master's and doctoral graduates.

Prepare for and take the Graduate Record Examination (GRE).

---

proving your note-taking skills is essential because accurate note taking is related to better test performance. Landrum and Davis (2007) offered some suggestions on how to improve your note-taking skills:

- Listen carefully to extract the most important information the lecturer is providing. Try to anticipate meanings and what is coming next.
- Review particularly difficult material in the text before the lecture.
- Do not try to record the exact words of the instructor. Take well-organized notes in your own words.
- Ask questions during the lecture. It is important to clarify information as you go along because often the material builds on itself. If you have misunderstood one point, it may be difficult to continue to follow the material presented.
- If the lecture is fast paced or if you take notes slowly, review your notes immediately after class and try to fill in what is missing.

TEST-TAKING SKILLS

Landrum and Davis (2007) suggested the following strategies for developing effective test-taking skills:

- Pace yourself. Be sure you are halfway through the test when half of the time is up.
- Do not waste a lot of time on difficult questions. Guess, and come back later if you have time.
- Do not make the test, or any particular question, more difficult than it is. Often questions are getting at the simpler meaning of things.
- Ask questions if you need clarification on an item.
- If you finish the entire test before time is up, review your test! Check for careless mistakes like missing an item.

Here are some tips for multiple-choice exams:

- As you read the question, anticipate the answer before you read the options.
- Even if you anticipated the answer, or if you think the first option is correct, read all the options. Choose the best answer.
- Eliminate implausible options. Often, you can narrow down the choices by eliminating options that are clearly not correct.
- Keep your eyes open for test questions that give away relevant information for one question in another question.
- Pay close attention to answer choices that are extra long. Detailed alternatives tend to be correct.
- Watch for key words such as *always, never, necessarily, only, must, completely,* and *totally.* Answer choices that create sweeping generalizations tend to be incorrect.
- Watch for words such as *often, sometimes, perhaps, may,* and *generally.* Options with carefully qualified statements are often correct.

Here are some tips for essay tests:

- Be sure to pace yourself. Time is typically critical in essay tests. Answer questions that you feel most confident with first. Be aware of the point values assigned to each question, and allocate your time and effort accordingly. Questions with higher point values will typically require longer, more detailed responses.
- Organize your thoughts and create a rough outline for your response.
- Be complete and concise in your response. Avoid the "kitchen-sink" method, where you don't know the answer but write down everything you do know about the topic in the hopes that the correct answer will be in there somewhere.
- Use specific terms and concepts that you have learned. You have likely learned a fair amount of jargon and terminology; be sure to use it (correctly) in your response to demonstrate your knowledge.

Develop Professional Relationships With Faculty

Get to know your professors. Sounds simple, doesn't it? You may even think that you already know your professors and that you do not need to read this section. Don't fool yourself. Knowing your professors, and making it your responsibility that they really know you, takes extra effort on your part. It may even take you out of your comfort zone. What does that mean? Initiating conversations with faculty and asking for advice or permission to join a research team can be intimidating and anxiety producing. You may have never done these kinds of things before, and you may have little to no confidence in your ability to do them effectively. Remember, the more experience you have with any given task or activity, the more self-confidence you will gain. Not only will your confidence grow, but you will become more skilled in communicating your interests and needs. So, approaching faculty is a risk worth taking.

How do you make yourself known to faculty? Talk with them after class and during their office hours. Ask questions and let them know what your interests are. You might ask them to supervise an independent study or to work with them on their research. At times, it is helpful to learn about your professors' career paths and how they got to be where they are now. As you can see, getting to know your professors is much more than simply attending class and ensuring that you know each other's names. Of course, you may not develop individual professional relationships with all of your professors, but consider the ones that seem most approachable and have professional interests the most similar to yours.

You may be wondering exactly what a professor can do for you or why developing a good professional relationship with faculty members might be helpful. Professors can introduce you to a world of opportunities and possibilities. They can involve students in research projects and introduce them to other faculty members. Professors also can help students network with other professionals to obtain practical experiences in the community, such as volunteer positions, internships, or summer jobs. Once faculty members get to know you better, they can provide you with more detailed letters of recommendation for graduate school or work opportunities. Detailed and personalized letters of recommendation that speak not only to course grades but also to your motivation, reliability, interpersonal skills, and other personal qualities will be more helpful than a general letter without much substance. Other roles that faculty can provide include advising and mentoring.

Faculty frequently play an academic advising role and assist students in choosing coursework that meets their requirements and matches their interests. Your advisor also can assist you by helping you to find other learning experiences to enrich your academic experience. Do not wait until you have a problem to see your advisor. Although your advisor can help you when you run into academic difficulties, he or she also is interested in helping you to get the most out of your undergraduate education in psychology. You will likely consult your advisor for big decisions like deciding whether or not to add or drop a course, change college majors, or transfer to another college or university. But remember to contact him or her at other times to keep the lines of communication open and to nurture your professional relationship.

There is much more you can gain from your professors. You can grow and learn from their experience as well as from the social support, role modeling, encouragement, and confidence in your abilities that they can provide. Exploring new domains like a college major and related work environments can be challenging. Having faculty who can support and encourage you will help you to navigate this uncharted territory with success. Advisors also sometimes provide a mentoring role for students. The importance of finding the right mentor, developing mentoring networks, and what to look for in a mentor, is discussed next.

Find a Mentor

A mentor is a professional who takes a special interest in you and your career and helps you to progress in various ways. A mentor is more than an advisor. Your mentor may be someone whom you admire and whom you would like to model your career after, someone who challenges you to take advantage of important opportunities, and someone who has your best interests at heart. He or she can serve as an advocate for you. Although faculty members are typical mentors for undergraduate psychology students, a number of professionals also could fulfill that role. For example, an internship supervisor or other community professional may provide you with a valuable mentoring experience.

Once you have a mentor, it is important to follow through on your commitments, be dependable, and maintain regular contact. You cannot just sit back and wait for your mentor to bring opportunities to you. The responsibility for your career ultimately rests with you. Tell your mentor what you would like to learn from him or her and be open to learning other things as well. Evidence suggests that students who are mentored are more satisfied with both their overall education and their education in psychology and are more productive in scholarly output (e.g., conference presentations, publications). Those who have been mentored also have reported feeling better prepared for either their current job or graduate school (Koch, 2002).

How do you find and choose the right mentor? Here is where the payoff really comes from getting to know your professors. If you know your professors and they really know you, it will be easier to choose one as a mentor. If you have done well in your coursework and have demonstrated that you are a motivated, committed, hard-working, and conscientious student, a faculty member may approach you to ask you to join his or her research team. But don't wait for this to happen. There is no substitute for approaching professors. It is always better to take the initiative. Talk to faculty about their interests and yours, complete internships, participate on faculty research teams, and engage in volunteer work either on-campus or in the community. How can a mentor be helpful? A mentor can help you to network and make connections, increase your professional opportunities, make you aware of available resources, increase your self-confidence, offer guidance and advice, and write letters of recommendation. Talk to your mentor about their career paths and share with them any concerns you have about your own career. The more professionals that you come into contact with the more likely it will be that you will meet someone who would be the right mentor for you. It also will benefit you to develop a mentoring network. Having more than one person to turn to for support and advice can be very helpful. How would you know whether someone would be the right mentor? There are a number of factors to consider.

A mentor who is right for you is a professional who has interests similar to yours, is approachable and easy to communicate with, is someone you get along with and perhaps admire, and has the time for and interest in mentoring you. A mentor is someone you can go to for advice and guidance on academic, personal, and career-related concerns and questions. Students often need encouragement and support to integrate their career and personal life goals. Therefore, it is important to choose a mentor whom you really feel comfortable talking to about these issues and with whom you can communicate easily and honestly. Professors who are actively involved in research that interests you are good candidates for mentors. Talk with them about your interests and their projects and communicate your desire to join their research team. The many benefits of joining a research team are discussed later in the chapter.

To develop the right mentoring network, you should be aware of your individual needs and career goals. Good questions to ask yourself include the following: What skills and abilities do I already possess? What type of professional do I want to become, and what skills and experiences do I have to obtain to do so? How can my college experience help me to bring about these changes? A good mentor can help you answer these questions (Appleby, 1999). Have a look at Table 6.1 for a list of desirable characteristics that successful mentors possess.

Some students prefer same-sex mentors (American Psychological Association [APA], 2007c). Similarly, students from underrepresented groups in psychology, such as racial and ethnic minorities, might prefer mentors from the same background to help them to integrate their racial and ethnic identity with their developing professional identity. Students also might look for faculty who are particularly sensitive and skilled at working with diverse students. There are other challenges and opportunities that may await you if you are a student from an underrepresented group in psychology (APA, 2007c). Chapter 7 of this volume includes a

TABLE 6.1

Characteristics of Successful Mentors

Characteristic	Components
Interpersonal skills	
Caring and encouraging	Empathic and nonjudgmental
	Facilitates the development of a positive self-concept
Promoting and sponsoring	Communicates positive aspects of protégé to others
	"Opens doors" to career and graduate school opportunities
Supporting and protecting	Source of emotional support
Challenging and demanding	Motivates protégés to attempt new tasks to stretch their abilities
	Unwilling to accept less-than-optimal performance
Personal attributes	
Mature and wise	Well-established in professional role
	Source of accurate and useful information
Friendly and optimistic	Genuinely enjoys the mentoring process
	Maintains a positive outlook on life
Admired and respected	Possesses characteristics that protégés aspire to
	Held in high regard by peers
Trustworthy and dependable	Possesses high ethical and moral standards
	Willing to provide assistance even under difficult conditions
Professional competencies	
Qualified and competent	Possesses necessary experiences and credentials
	Capable and effective professional
Experienced and seasoned	Possesses valuable experiences and is willing to share them
Knowledgeable and informative	Possesses accurate up-to-date information
	Able and willing to communicate information to protégés
Professionally involved and active	Actively involved in professional or academic organizations
	Adheres to a philosophy of lifelong learning

Note. From "Choosing a Mentor," by D. Appleby, 1999, *Eye on Psi Chi, 3*(3), pp. 38–39. Copyright 1999 by Psi Chi. Adapted with permission.

discussion about this as well as the need for people from diverse backgrounds to enter the field of psychology.

Engage in Research

Students can get involved in research by either assisting professors with their research or by initiating an independent research project. Most students begin by getting experience assisting faculty. This helps students to develop research skills that can later be applied to independent projects.

Why should you get involved in research? Conducting research facilitates the application of classroom and textbook knowledge and increases your understanding of the concepts that you learn in class. It also helps you to develop your analytical and critical thinking skills and offers a collaborative work experience. Engaging in research with a professor can foster a mentoring relationship (Koch, 2002). Take a look at Exhibit 6.3 for other advantages to serving as a research assistant. Exhibit 6.4 offers a glimpse at some of the actual tasks that you might likely be doing. Students interested in seeking research opportunities should also frequent the APA Division 2 (Society for the Teaching of Psychology) Web site at http://www.teachpsych.org, which provides a link to publications and awards for undergraduate students.

An exciting aspect of engaging in research is that it often leads to the dissemination of the results through professional presentations at conferences and publications in scholarly journals. Some students might have the opportunity to participate in research symposiums or compete in research colloquia at their university. For others, their first experience presenting research findings might occur at a regional or state conference. More experienced students, or those taking an active role in a larger research project, also might have the opportunity to present their work at a national conference. Attending conferences and presenting your work affords you the opportunity to meet faculty and peers with similar interests and gain contacts to further those interests; it also opens doors to new opportunities.

Most psychological organizations, like APA or state and regional psychological associations, have annual conferences. Conference presentations typically are in one of two formats: posters or papers. Poster presentations are the most common type of presentation for undergraduate students. In a poster presentation, your work is displayed concisely on a 3×5 or 4×6–foot freestanding bulletin board. During these sessions, all posters are displayed for a predetermined amount of time (typically an hour). Observers walk past each poster presentation and read the sum-

EXHIBIT 6.3

Advantages of Serving as a Research Assistant

Developing skills and knowledge not easily gained in the classroom

Working one-on-one with a faculty member

Contributing to advancements in the science of psychology

Gaining exposure to general research techniques helpful for pursuing later graduate work

Developing verbal communication skills by preparing and presenting at professional conferences

Improving writing skills by preparing and submitting manuscripts for publication

Cultivating mentoring relationships with faculty; helpful for acquiring letters of recommendation

Note. From Landrum and Davis (2004).

maries of the work displayed. During this process, there is ample opportunity to engage in discussions about your work. Participation in poster sessions provides a fruitful opportunity to network with faculty and students with similar professional interests.

Paper presentations typically consist of a 12-minute to 15-minute verbal presentation of your work. Overheads or slides are often used as visual aids for the presentation. Paper presentations are often grouped together in a symposium in which three or four people present papers followed by a discussant who offers comments on the work presented. Symposia are typically organized by one or two people, who then invite others to present papers on a similar topic or theme. Individual paper presentations that are not part of a symposium can be from 60 minutes to 75 minutes in length, allowing you to go into much more detail.

As a research assistant, you may have the opportunity to assist in preparing a manuscript for submission to a scholarly journal. The *Psi Chi Journal of Undergraduate Research* is one popular option for the publication of undergraduate research, but many other journals exist. Faculty will teach you how to match the topic of your research to the appropriate scholarly journal. Once you submit your manuscript to a journal for review, the editor of the journal typically distributes it to three anonymous reviewers. It then usually takes several months for the reviews to be completed and for you to receive notification on whether your manuscript has been accepted for publication. Most manuscripts accepted for publication require revision and resubmission, and not all manuscripts are accepted for publication. Publishing in a scholarly journal is an admirable achievement that is highly valued by graduate schools and employers.

EXHIBIT 6.4

Typical Tasks of a Research Assistant

Collect data by administering surveys or conducting interviews.

Score data and enter into a data file for statistical analysis (using a program such as SPSS).

Conduct computer literature searches (using resources such as PsycINFO), photocopy articles, order unavailable articles and books through interlibrary loan.

Work with faculty and/or a research team on developing new research ideas.

Attend research team meetings to discuss progress on research projects.

Use computer software, such as word processing, spreadsheet, scheduling, and statistical analysis programs.

Prepare results to be submitted for presentation and publication.

Collaborate with faculty and members of the research team.

Seek Out Field Experiences and Internships

Field experiences and internships offer an opportunity to apply psychological principles to real people in real situations. Not only do you benefit from your experiences, but through your efforts you can provide useful services to the community. Universities often refer to this as *service learning* and sometimes require it of their graduates. Field experiences tend to include placements in community agencies, schools, hospitals, or specialized residential or day treatment programs. The experiences that you can gain from these placements range from participant observations to more active participation such as assisting with psychoeducational groups or test administration. Some of your psychology courses might require field observations. For example, a developmental psychology course might require observations at a day care center, an abnormal psychology course might include observations of an inpatient psychiatry unit, or a psychology of aging course could require nursing home observations. Observing people interact in different settings gives real-world meaning to what you are learning in the classroom.

An internship, compared with a field experience, might provide you with more responsibilities and opportunities to become involved in the tasks and routines typical of mental health professionals. For example, you might get experience conducting structured intake interviews or participating in multidisciplinary team meetings. Internships also offer opportunities to learn more about potential careers and work settings. By interacting with a variety of professionals, you will learn about various career options and educational requirements. Internships provide valuable on-the-job experience that can be helpful in deciding which careers are, and are not, for you. These experiences can facilitate the development of professional and personal confidence, responsibility, and maturity (LoCicero & Hancock, 2000). Participation in internships also allows students to meet contacts that could be beneficial to them in the future.

Get Involved in Student and Professional Organizations

Becoming involved in student and professional organizations is an excellent way to socialize yourself into the field of psychology. It provides numerous opportunities to develop leadership skills, which have been largely overlooked in undergraduate psychology programs. Although psychologists have been at the forefront in studying leadership, few have applied these principles to the development of future leaders in the field (Sternberg, 2005). Although many psychologists become effective leaders in their professional careers, few have had formal coursework or training in leadership. Leadership as a content area has traditionally been covered in business schools and departments of educational administration. As an undergraduate psychology student, you might try expanding your horizons by taking coursework outside of your major to gain additional knowledge and skills that will help you become a more effective leader in your field.

A good organization to become involved with is your institution's chapter of Psi Chi, the National Honor Society in Psychology. Psi Chi is a student organization that was founded in 1929 to encourage, stimulate, and maintain excellence in scholarship and advance the science of psychology. This organization has two major goals: to provide academic recognition to its inductees by meeting the qualifications for membership and to nourish and stimulate professional growth through programs designed to augment the regular curriculum and provide practical experience through affiliation with the chapter. Students must meet the minimum qualifications to become a member. Eligibility for undergraduate students includes (a) completion of three semesters or five quarters of college study, (b) completion of 9 semester hours or 14 quarter hours of psychology courses, (c) ranking in the top 35% of their class in general scholarship, and (d) a minimum grade point average of 3.0 (on a 4.0

scale) in both psychology courses and in cumulative grades (Psi Chi, 2002–2007). To become a member, students must be enrolled at an institution that has a chapter of Psi Chi. If your college or university is not a member institution, think about taking the lead and making it a member institution. For further information about starting a chapter, refer to the Psi Chi Web site (http://www.psichi.org/about/start_chapter.asp).

By becoming a member of Psi Chi, you will have the opportunity to get to know other psychology students in an informal setting, develop leadership skills, develop and nurture a professional identity, and become involved in departmental activities. Psi Chi also offers you the opportunity to become involved in regional and national events. The organization typically sponsors programs at regional and national conferences to promote the research and scholarship of undergraduate psychology students. Conference programming provided by Psi Chi typically concerns topics of interest to undergraduates, such as careers in psychology and tips on applying to graduate school.

Psi Chi publishes a quarterly newsletter that provides a forum for recognizing student contributions and accomplishments, and other helpful information on how to get the most out of your undergraduate experience. I have mentioned Psi Chi's national peer-reviewed journal; take a look at it and consider it as a potential outlet for your work. There are a number of other benefits to becoming a member of Psi Chi, such as competitive research awards to support undergraduate research. Check out their Web site to learn more about this organization (http://www.psichi.org).

Psi Beta is Psi Chi's sister honor society for community and junior colleges. The mission of the Psi Beta National Honor Society in Psychology for Community and Junior Colleges is to promote the professional development of psychology students in 2-year colleges by encouraging and recognizing excellence in scholarship, leadership, research, and community service. Psi Beta provides opportunities to interact with faculty outside of the classroom, learn more about the professional and educational options available, meet peers with similar interests, and receive the organization's newsletter published twice a year. Opportunities also are available to participate in national, regional, and local psychological association programs and presentations.

Students who are enrolled in an accredited 2-year college with a Psi Beta chapter are eligible to become a member if they meet certain minimal requirements. Students must rank in the top 35% or have an overall grade point average of 3.0 (in a 4.0 system), have at least a B average in psychology courses, have completed at least two quarters or one semester of a psychology or psychology-based course and 12 semester hours (or the equivalent quarter hours) total college credit, have demonstrated a genuine interest in psychology and high standards of personal behavior and integrity, have been approved by the chapter and received a written invitation to membership, have signed a completed membership registration card accepting Psi Beta's bylaws and policies, and have paid the one-time national registration fee. For more information about this organization, consult their Web site (http://www.psibeta.org/).

Many psychology departments have psychology clubs that are open to any student with an interest in psychology. Students who do not meet the minimum qualifications for membership in Psi Chi often get involved in a psychology club. Psychology clubs frequently coordinate their efforts with Psi Chi to organize collaborative events and activities.

Students also should consider joining professional organizations such as the APA. Undergraduate students are eligible to become student affiliate members of APA. A student affiliate membership allows you to obtain discounts on journals and books and attend the annual APA national convention at a reduced rate. Attending conferences sponsored by professional organizations, whether or not you make a presentation, is a good way to learn about the field, start thinking about psychology subfields, and meet people with similar interests.

Become Active in Extracurricular and Volunteer Activities

Involvement in campus and community activities and organizations sends a message to employers and graduate admissions committees. It communicates that you are a person who is interested in making a contribution to your community. Being involved in campus and community projects also provides a vehicle to help others, to meet people who have different interests and are from different backgrounds, and to diversify your skills (including team building, problem solving, and communication skills). It is yet another way to expand your network and develop leadership potential. When you apply for graduate school or a job, you can use all of these experiences to demonstrate the skills, characteristics, and knowledge that you have gained.

Broaden Your Horizons: International Psychology

The world is rapidly changing. The psychology of the future is likely to be more global and culturally inclusive than the psychology of today (Hogan & Gielen, 2004). Technological advances, political changes, and economic forces (e.g., globalization) have led to increased interconnection across the globe. As the interdependence of people continues to increase, it becomes even more important to develop an understanding of cultures other than one's own. See chapter 7 of this volume for a discussion of the many ways in which diversity can enhance and broaden psychology's effectiveness. College graduates with a rich knowledge of people from other nations and diverse cultural perspectives find that they are well equipped to profit from the opportunities and challenges in today's world. For psychology students, a clear understanding of the differences between various cultures, and a respect for diverse worldviews, is essential. How can you learn more about international psychology? Here are a few tips from Hogan and Gielen (2004) as well as a few additional ones:

- Join APA Division 52 (International Psychology) as a student affiliate and receive their quarterly newsletter. To get additional information and to download a membership form, go to the division Web site (http://orgs.tamu-commerce.edu/div52/membership.htm).
- Join APA Division 45 (Society for the Study of Ethnic Minority Issues) as a student affiliate and receive the division publications *Focus* and the quarterly journal *Cultural Diversity and Ethnic Minority Psychology.* For more information, see the division Web site (http://www.apa.org/divisions/div45/).
- Read the quarterly newsletter published by the International Affairs Office of the American Psychological Association in collaboration with the Committee on International Relations in Psychology (CIRP). Learn more about what is going on in the International Affairs Office of APA, and download the newsletter called *Psychology International* from the office's Web site (http://www.apa.org/international).
- Consider joining an international psychology professional organization as a student member. Three prominent international psychology organizations (together with their respective Web site addresses) are the International Association of Applied Psychology (IAAP; http://www.iaapsy.org), the International Council of Psychologists (ICP; http://icpsych.tripod.com), and the International Association for Cross-Cultural Psychology (IACCP; http://www.iaccp.org). The many benefits of membership include contact and interaction with psychologists and students from other nations who are interested in international issues and concerns. Some international organizations offer funding opportunities for research and travel to conferences. Memberships also provide access to newsletters and other publications sponsored by the organizations.
- Read international psychology journals. Several prominent international psychology journals include *European Psychologist, Applied*

Psychology: An International Review, and the *International Journal of Psychology.*

■ Review the invited addresses of award winners of the APA Award for the International Advancement of Psychology. Every year, the Committee of International Relations in Psychology presents the APA Award for the International Advancement of Psychology to an outstanding American or International Psychologist. The invited addresses of the award winners are published annually in the *American Psychologist.* Reading these invited addresses will help you to better understand some of the important issues, research findings, and theoretical frameworks infused in recent work in international psychology.

■ Take a course on cross-cultural psychology. If your department does not offer a cross-cultural psychology course, consider doing an independent study or enrolling in an online course from another university.

■ Read books and articles on cross-cultural and international psychology. Explore psychological topics that incorporate international perspectives and cross-cultural themes. See the reading list at the end of the chapter for some suggestions.

■ Consider becoming involved in an international research project. Find out if any of the psychology faculty in your department are involved in international research, but don't stop there. Faculty members in other departments at your college or university may be engaged in international collaborations. Do some investigating. Stop by your institution's office for international services and programs to find out what resources are available.

■ Consider future international research opportunities as you are exploring graduate school options. As you begin to explore graduate programs in psychology, look for faculty interested in international scholarship.

■ Consider studying abroad or hosting an international student. Integrating cultural immersion and formal training in international psychology (through the curriculum) are important to the development of personal and professional skills necessary for successful international work. Cultural immersion provides students with information about other cultures and the skills to incorporate and use this knowledge effectively (McCaslin, 2003). Research has suggested that students traveling abroad grow significantly in their personal development (Gmelch, 1997; Martin & Rohrlich, 1991). Exposure to a culture different from one's own facilitates the development of adaptability, self-confidence, and self-reliance. An openness to learn and share your knowledge with international

colleagues will make your international experience both personally and professionally enriching.

Summary

The opportunities to put more into, and get more out of, your undergraduate education in psychology are endless. They may even seem a
little overwhelming. The good news is that much of the needed effort
can be boiled down to developing good relationships with your professors, who can then guide you in your journey. Most students find the
undergraduate years both enriching and challenging. It is up to you to
take the lead in creating a balance between the two. Refer back to chapter 4 for guidance on how to approach the many decisions you will face
throughout your education and career.

Suggested Web Sites

- Become a Member of Psi Chi. This site provides information about
  becoming a member of the Psi Chi National Honor Society in Psychology: http://www.psichi.org/about/becomember.asp
- Psi Beta. Psi Beta is an honor society in psychology for community
  and junior colleges: http://www.psibeta.org
- *Eye on Psi Chi.* This online magazine is published by the National
  Honor Society in Psychology. Eye on Psi Chi features informative
  articles about careers, graduate school admission, chapter ideas,
  personal development, the various fields of psychology, and important issues related to the discipline. See http://www.psichi.org/
  pubs/eye/home.asp
- APA Student Page. Information and resources for psychology students: http://www.apa.org/students/
- Become a Student Affiliate Member of APA. If you are a graduate
  or undergraduate student taking courses in psychology, you are
  eligible to become an APA Student Affiliate: http://www.apa.org/
  membership/forstudents.html
- Become a Student Affiliate Member of APA Division 52 (International Psychology). You will receive their quarterly newsletter with
  membership: http://orgs.tamu-commerce.edu/div52/membership.htm
- APA International Affairs Office. Information about psychology in
  the international setting: http://www.apa.org/international

■ Become a Student Affiliate Member of APA Division 45 (Society for the Study of Ethnic Minority Issues). You will receive the division publications *Focus* and the quarterly journal *Cultural Diversity and Ethnic Minority Psychology* with membership: http://www.apa.org/divisions/div45/

Suggested Reading

Arnett, J. J. (2002). The psychology of globalization. *American Psychologist, 57,* 774–783.

Landrum, R. E., & Davis, S. F. (2007). *The psychology major: Career options and strategies for success* (3rd ed.). Upper Saddle River, NJ: Pearson Prentice Hall.

Wedding, D., & Stevens, M. (Eds.). (2004). *The handbook of international psychology.* New York: Brunner-Routledge.

Strength in Diversity 7

The strength of multicultural diversity in psychology is in its potential to enhance and broaden psychology's effectiveness. Just as you were encouraged to broaden your horizons in chapter 6 of this volume, in the current chapter you will learn more about the importance of understanding and appreciating diverse cultures. Diversity is valuable in promoting and opening up new ways of thinking, teaching, learning, conducting research, and solving problems (Wiley, 2001). When we speak of diversity, we mean differences in such things as race or ethnicity, gender, disability status, age, religion, or sexual orientation. Psychologists from heterogeneous groups across the globe bring new insights to the needs of underserved populations. It is not only important to have psychologists who are minorities but also to have psychologists who are interested, respectful, and nonjudgmental about diversity issues. Ethnic minority psychologists are more likely to offer diverse perspectives that can help generate the development of alternative theories in psychology that are relevant for ethnic minority clientele, applicable to contemporary social issues, and congruent with the field's commitment to social justice (Vasquez & Jones, 2006). At a time when there is a pressing need for competent ethnically diverse researchers, educators, and practitioners to serve an increasingly diverse clientele and student body, persons of color are underrepresented in psychology. It is in everyone's best interests to address this problem.

Diversity in education benefits all members of society, not just ethnic minorities (Crosby & Clayton, 2001). Gender, ethnic–racial, and cultural differences play a vital role in the intellectual life of a university. Experiences with diverse groups on college campuses can be valuable in promoting openness and interest in other racial and ethnic groups and in learning how to live and work more effectively with members of other races (Crosby & Clayton, 2001). These experiences also can promote thinking in pluralistic and complex ways and nurture a commitment to lifelong learning about diversity (Gurin, Nagda, & Lopez, 2004).

This chapter provides a discussion of issues relevant to the participation of racial and ethnic minority students in psychology, the infusion of a multicultural perspective across the undergraduate psychology curriculum, the development of self-awareness, the harmful effects of stereotyping, and culturally sensitive patterns of interaction and communication. To help you understand the strength of diversity in psychology, a series of exercises are provided throughout the chapter to promote self-reflection.

Racial and Ethnic Minority Students in Psychology

Minority students of color are underrepresented at all levels of psychology but most notably at the doctoral level and among psychology faculty (Maton, Kohout, Wicherski, Leary, & Vinokurov, 2006). *Minority students of color* refers to persons who identify as Black/African American, Latino/a, Asian American, American Indian, Pacific Islander, and biracial or mixed ethnic background. There have been both promising and disconcerting trends in minority student enrollment and graduation rates. Between 1989 and 2002, the percentage of minority psychology students receiving the bachelor's degree steadily increased (from 13.6% in 1989 to 24.3% in 2002), as did the percentage receiving the master's degree (from 10.6% in 1989 to 21.5% in 2002). The trend for minority psychology students receiving the doctoral degree was less promising. From 1989 to 2000, receipt of the doctoral degree among minority students increased from 8.0% to 15.7% but has not increased since. Moreover, the percentage of African American and Latino/a students entering PhD programs has not changed since 1997 (Maton et al., 2006). These trends have occurred during a time of dramatic change in the ethnic makeup of the U.S. population. Between 1990 and 2000, the percentage of Whites in the United States decreased from 75.6% to 69.4%, whereas the percentage of persons of Hispanic origin increased from 9.0% to 12.6% (U.S. Census Bureau, 2002).

Efforts are under way to increase the numbers of racial and ethnic minorities at all levels of psychology, from the undergraduate major in psychology to doctoral level training. Creation of a welcoming and supportive environment that encourages retention of minority students through graduation has been shown to be effective in increasing minority student recruitment and retention. Successful programs have been known to (a) contain a sizeable number of students of color, (b) provide students with opportunities to collaborate with faculty on diversity issues and research, (c) offer at least one diversity issues course, (d) have faculty who are involved in a wide array of campus-based diversity initiatives, and (e) have faculty who perceived that their commitment to recruiting and retaining minority students of color was supported within the broader institutional environment (Rogers & Molina, 2006).

Undergraduate minority students are encouraged to find faculty and student allies who share in the goals of promoting diversity (Vasquez et al., 2006). Such allies help reduce isolation, provide assistance in new environments, buffer the stress of difference, serve as role models, and help counter stereotypes. They also help counter barriers such as limited perceptions of opportunity and discrimination (Cockley, Dreher, & Stockdale, 2004; Xu & Leffler, 1996). A significant number of minority faculty increases perceptions that the department will provide respect and openness to all cultural backgrounds and that the faculty will be trusted and valued as mentors and role models (Maton et al., 2006). Faculty who hold positive beliefs in the capacity of persons of color to achieve provide encouragement to students and have constructive and empowering effects (Vasquez et al., 2006).

Curriculum That Infuses a Multicultural Perspective

Although there may well be a specific course at your college or university that is devoted to multicultural diversity, each psychology course that you take will relate to diversity in one way or another. How? Well, understanding human behavior requires examining the ways in which individuals and society understand and interpret the meaning of differences and the issues of power and privilege that coincide with these meanings (American Psychological Association, 2003). For example, you might find that your history of psychology course includes discussions of the contributions of people who have been left out of historical accounts of psychology including women, people of color, and lesbian, gay, and bisexual individuals. Have a look at Table 7.1 for a few other ways that multicultural issues are integrated into two select courses, life span development and abnormal psychology.

TABLE 7.1

Infusion of Multicultural Content Into Two Typical Undergraduate Psychology Courses

Course	Topic and examples of content
Life span development	**Culture, ethnicity, and race** • Emphasis on the variability of development and the social, cultural, and economic factors that affect such variability. • Discussion of the idea that ecological theories of human development and stage theories are culturally dependent. • Discussion of cultural variability in child-rearing practices. **Gender** • Differentiations between sex and gender and acknowledgement that gendered roles differ across cultures. • Discussions of how parent and caregiver expectations are stereotyped in most cultures for gendered behavior and challenges to assumptions that sex differences in behavior are innate. **Sexual orientation** • Challenges to the prevailing assumption that heterosexuality is the normative outcome of psychosexual development. • Challenges LGB people face because of heterosexism; the process of coming out or developing a LGB identity, noting how this process varies by life stage, interactions with other facets of identity (i.e., ethnic, racial, gender, disability).
Abnormal psychology	**Culture, ethnicity, and race** • Effects of racism and discrimination on coping behaviors and personality, how coping can adversely affect behavioral and psychological functioning, and how resilience and psychological strength can help lessen the effects of a hostile social climate. • The idea that many ethnic and cultural groups have not been offered the opportunity to provide their perspective on what "abnormal" means from their cultural worldview and how many cultural groups have their own cultural-specific descriptions for abnormal behavior. **Disability** • Emphasis on the ways that bias occurs in the diagnosis of people with disabilities. • Emphasis on the strength, resilience, and adaptability found in people with disabilities.

Gender
- Differential rates of diagnoses between men and women.
- Inclusion of feminist psychological perspectives and discussions that examine the role of the social factors in predisposing either men or women to present with specific disorders with greater or lesser frequency.
- Examination of the ways women's subordinate social status and traditional gender roles may contribute adversely to women's optimal mental health.

Note. Material in this table is adapted from Trimble, Stevenson, Worell, and the APA Commission on Ethnic Minority Recruitment, Retention, and Training Task Force Textbook Initiative Work Group (2003). LGB = lesbian, gay, bisexual.

Self-Awareness: The First Step Toward Developing Multicultural Competence

All people are shaped by the cultures in which they are raised, including those who consider themselves to be members of the dominant U.S. culture. *Multicultural competence* refers to an appreciation of different cultures as well as the knowledge, skills, and sensitivity to interact with people who are different from you. Culture is more than race, ethnicity, and gender; it includes religion, age, sexual orientation, disability status, socioeconomic status, and so on. It can also include differences in values, beliefs, language, communication styles, and many other factors. Whether you plan to work immediately after college or to attend graduate school, in today's global society you will need to interact with people from diverse cultural groups. Success in a diverse workplace is dependent on a personal and social style characterized by a willingness and ability to work with others. Diversity creates new opportunities for growth and learning for all workers (Blocher, Heppner, & Johnston, 2001).

As a psychology major, you will learn to understand diversity without judging and will develop a sensitivity and appreciation of differences. You will also learn how to establish trust, to listen to others who think and feel differently than you, and to work effectively with people from cultures that are vastly different from your own. Learning to adapt and grow in a multicultural world can be both the biggest challenge and the greatest opportunity of your undergraduate career and working life. Even if you do not ultimately choose a career in psychology, the development of multicultural knowledge, skills, and self-awareness will benefit you in whichever career path you choose and across many other aspects of your personal and social life.

EXHIBIT 7.1

Exercise 1: Recognizing Difference

The purpose of this exercise is to help you to identify and process your experiences of being different from others around you. Think about a time you came to realize that your way of life was not the same as everyone else's. What did you notice? Was it a behavior, a ritual, a belief, implicit or explicit family rules, foods, holidays? How did you feel? What were your thoughts about yourself and your way of life and your thoughts about the other person and his or her way of life? Once you discovered these differences, did you change your behavior or thoughts? If so, how? What implications, if any, did your realization of these differences have on your interactions with others who you perceived to be different or the same as you?

To learn more about your own personal response to differences, it might be helpful to call to mind the times when you have perceived yourself to be different in some way. Try Exercise 1 (Exhibit 7.1) to explore your earliest experience with this. Once you have completed this exercise, try Exercise 2 (Exhibit 7.2) to reflect further on your unique cultural heritage.

The path toward multicultural competence begins with self-exploration and the development of self-awareness. It is important to first develop a good understanding of your cultural heritage and personal worldview. The term *worldview* refers to one's basic perceptions and understandings of the world (Sue & Sue, 1990). This includes views about human nature, family, intimate and social relationships, time, space, and activities such as work. Your worldview provides a frame of reference through which you experience the world and serves as a basis for your beliefs, attitudes, and relationships. Thinking about how your worldview differs from that of others can help you understand some of the ways that people differ in relation to their cultural heritage. Psychologists' worldviews shape psychological theory, research questions, the content and nature of program curricula, and the services that psychologists provide. How do you see the world? How would you describe your worldview? Try writing about it in Exercise 3 (Exhibit 7.3).

Contextual Factors Influencing Worldview

Socioeconomic status is more than the amount of money a person has. It includes a whole set of behaviors, values, and ideas about life's possibili-

EXHIBIT 7.2

Exercise 2: Promoting a Multicultural Self-Awareness

The purpose of this exercise is to help you to become more aware of the diverse cultural groups to which you belong and that influence who you are. Think about all of the different cultural influences in your life, including your ethnic heritage from your parents and grandparents; your gender, religion, race, socioeconomic class; and other reference groups. Think about how these cultural influences shaped your sense of self, family relationships, gender roles, educational and work expectations, values, and outlook on life. What messages did you receive? What did you learn about what to expect from life?

ties that shape one's worldview (Okun, Fried, & Okun, 1999). Socioeconomic status affects a person's hope for the future and sense of the possibilities that life has to offer, including his or her choice of work or career. People of a higher socioeconomic status more often believe that they have choices and possibilities compared with people of a lower socioeconomic status. When mere survival is an issue, anything that contributes to that goal is enough (Okun et al., 1999). Thus, socioeconomic status deeply affects whether someone thinks in terms of choosing a specific career or is grateful just to have the best-paying job available. How have socioeconomic status, gender, and race shaped who you are? Complete Exercise 4 (Exhibit 7.4) to help you to explore these issues further.

Stereotypes and Biases

In addition to learning about yourself, majoring in psychology will help you learn more about stereotypes and biases. *Stereotyping* is a representation of a category of persons that tends to be inaccurate and to exaggerate real differences and the perception of those differences (Okun et al., 1999). Stereotyping occurs when we focus on only one or two characteristics of the other person, often membership in a particular social or racial group. In focusing on these aspects, we begin to attribute assumed characteristics, motives, or beliefs to the person—whether or not the individual's actual behavior, accomplishments, or intentions are consistent with those characteristics. Stereotyping hurts others and distances us from them, making it difficult to empathize (Blocher et al., 2001). Racism, sexism, ageism, and heterosexism are all forms of prejudice. Prejudice arises from the belief that one group of people is morally superior to another and therefore deserves power and privilege. Prejudice can lead to unconscious attitudes of superiority, entitlement, and privilege, as well

EXHIBIT 7.3

Exercise 3: What Is Your Worldview?

How do you see the world? What assumptions do you hold about what to expect in life? How do you view human nature—as inherently good or evil or a combination of both? How do you view social relationships (as hierarchical, group oriented, or individualistic)? What is your perspective of time? Are you focused on the past, the present, or the future? What do you value? After considering these aspects of your worldview, consider how your worldview affects your daily life. How might it affect your future job? What would it be like for you to work with someone with a worldview that is vastly different from yours?

as a failure to listen to and to learn from others with different cultural heritages.

Stereotyping also can occur with regard to occupations. People often hold stereotypes about people from various occupational groups. These stereotypes have many of the same dangers as stereotypes that lead to prejudice and discrimination, but they also can lead to occupational circumscription. *Occupational circumscription* is the progressive elimination from consideration of occupations on the basis of some unacceptable stereotype that does not fit with one's view of oneself. The most common stereotype is gender stereotyping. Many people rule out the possibility of exploring certain careers because they have not traditionally been associated with their gender. For example, several decades ago, many men would not have considered being a flight attendant or a nurse and many women would not have considered a career in management. Occupational stereotyping occurs with regard to racial–ethnic groups and socioeconomic status as well. What's your stereotype of a psychologist? Try completing Exercise 5 (Exhibit 7.5) to learn more about your stereotype.

Culturally Sensitive Patterns of Interaction and Communication

Studying psychology will help you appreciate the effects of culture on communication. For example, people from different cultural groups vary in terms of how much personal space they need and whether they make eye contact. You also will learn to recognize and modify your physical and verbal communication style and understand how your communication style interacts with the style of others. As you develop self-awareness,

EXHIBIT 7.4

Exercise 4: Socioeconomic Status, Gender, and Race

The purpose of this exercise is to explore how your beliefs have been shaped by these factors and how they might influence your career choice. Think about how your socioeconomic status, gender, race, and ethnicity have shaped your major beliefs about what job or career you will ultimately pursue. How do your beliefs fit with your view of what psychology is and has to offer? Do Western views that have historically predominated U.S. psychology fit with your beliefs about what career would be best for you? Has learning about all that psychology has to offer, including a future shaped by enhanced diversity and broadened global horizons, changed your views about this? If so, how? What types of compromises would you have to make? What types of changes would you hope to see in the field to fit with your beliefs? What would you need to feel supported in having your opinions heard in the world of psychology?

an awareness of others, and culturally sensitive interpersonal skills, you will begin to be able to (a) separate facts from cultural assumptions and beliefs about those facts, (b) shift between your own cultural perspective and your understanding of others' cultural perspectives, and (c) differentiate between personal discomfort and intellectual disagreement (see, e.g., Okun et al., 1999).

Accurate perception and interpretation of patterns of interaction are crucial in defining and maintaining personal, social, and work relationships (Okun et al., 1999). The way we experience and display emotion is influenced by culture. Even humor is culturally defined. What one person finds humorous may be no laughing matter to another. Communication is culturally embedded. It involves both verbal and nonverbal components. When we listen to another person talk, we do more than simply listen to the content of his or her words. Effective communication means perceiving and understanding what is being communicated both verbally and nonverbally. The tone, volume, and pacing of speech; distance between the speaker and listener; the amount of physical touching, eye contact, body movements; and facial expressions are all important components of nonverbal communication.

Someone who is culturally sensitive is aware of how one's expectations regarding patterns of behavior and communication are based on comfort with one's own style and the unique styles of others. Flexibility and adaptability are important hallmarks of good communicators. Effective communicators also understand cultural norms regarding which topics of conversation are considered appropriate in different social situations. One of the biggest challenges facing people across the globe is learning how to communicate with people from different cultural, ethnic, racial,

Exercise 5: Stereotypes and Biases

The purpose of this exercise is to sensitize you to the power of stereotypes. Think for a minute about your stereotype of a psychologist. What image comes to mind? What characteristics does this professional have? How similar are this person's assumed characteristics to yours? How do you feel as you think about the differences between your perceived characteristics and those that you assume a psychologist would have? What implications, if any, does your realization of these differences have on your career plans?

religious, and socioeconomic backgrounds. Being a good communicator means having both good listening skills and good speaking skills. As a psychology major, you will learn the communication skills necessary for success. You will learn about your own personal communication styles and how they vary in different contexts and relationships. You also will become aware of others' communication styles and patterns of interaction. Learning how we communicate both verbally and nonverbally is an important step toward learning how to communicate effectively across cultures. Complete Exercise 6 (Exhibit 7.6) to gain more information about your communication style. To learn more about the implicit roles of communication, try Exercise 7 (Exhibit 7.7).

Summary

Honest discussions about the challenges and opportunities in the profession of psychology can help you decide what you have to offer to this growing and dynamic field. Learning from psychologists of color who are willing to share their personal experiences with others is one way that you can benefit from others' experiences and strengths. Professionals are often willing to pass on their knowledge so that you can learn from their struggles and make a different life for yourself (Vasquez & Reyes, 2004). See Exhibit 7.8 for an outline of challenges and strategies for success, confidence, and well-being outlined by prominent psychologists of color (Vasquez & Reyes, 2004). Additional insightful resources are available in the Suggested Reading section of this chapter to help you on your journey of self-discovery and decision making as you learn how leaders in the field have negotiated challenges.

The profession of psychology must keep pace with demographic changes in the United States and the globalization of our world economy.

EXHIBIT 7.6

Exercise 6: What Kind of Communicator Are You, Anyway?

Think about your personal communication style. Are you a good listener? Do you communicate clearly and concisely? Does your nonverbal communication match your verbal communication? Do you say what is on your mind? Do you offer your opinions and beliefs to others whether they have asked for them or not? Are you assertive, passive, or aggressive in your communication? After you have given some thought to how you perceive yourself as a communicator, ask three people who know you well what type of a communicator they think you are. Are their views consistent with each other and with your own? If not, why do you think that is so? Have you learned anything about your communication style? If so, how do you feel about what you have learned? Will it change how you communicate at all?

EXHIBIT 7.7

Exercise 7: Dinnertime Rules

The purpose of this exercise is to heighten your awareness about explicit and implicit rules and messages about communication. Think about what it is like to sit at your dinner table with your family. What communication styles do you notice? Does only one person talk at a time? Does everyone listen to the person who is talking? Is the conversation typically directed toward or away from certain people? What and how do people communicate without speaking? What tones of voice are used? Now, remember a time when you sat at another person's family dinner table. What was that like? How was the communication similar and different? How did you feel about differences you perceived? Once you discovered these differences, did you change your behavior or thoughts? If so, how? What implications, if any, did your realization of these differences have on your interactions with others?

EXHIBIT 7.8

Challenges to Success and Strategies for Success, Confidence, and Well-Being

Challenges to Success: External

■ Discrimination is more likely to occur when competition for jobs or promotion occurs with those who hold similar qualifications (e.g., highly qualified Blacks with highly qualified Whites; highly qualified women with highly qualified men; Jones, 1996).

continues

- Racism among Whites is subtle, often unintentional and unconscious, but its effects are systematically damaging to race relations by fostering miscommunication and distrust (Dovidio, Gaertner, Kawakami, & Hodson, 2002).
- Lack of mentoring and support can be lonely.
- The backlash that exists in society to the few gains that women and minorities have made is pervasive, including in the profession of psychology.
- The perception that the contributions of women and ethnic minorities aren't as valued.

Challenges to Success: Internal

- Socialization of women and ethnic minorities often leads to a lack of confidence and a fear of risk taking in uncharted territories.
- Internalized oppression may cause one to question the viability of one's own or others' ability to perform well in a variety of activities related to success.

Strategies for Success, Confidence, and Well-Being

- Take risks—allow curiosity and energy to give direction to areas you wish to explore.
- Allow for imperfections and mistakes—learn from them and move on.
- Understand that emotional pain is a part of life—learn to cope in healthy ways by getting support and using other healthy options.
- Focus on areas about which you have passion—our natural talents tend to come to the forefront when we work in areas that we love or about which we have interest or energy.
- Be persistent—persistence is one of the major qualities that employers, admissions committees, and others assess in selection processes.
- Network—success can come from positive connections with people.
- Develop skills and confidence—these skills of how to express your perspective assertively, how to articulate your ideas, how to face creative conflict in order to reach resolutions will help you in your education and in your life.
- Find activities and projects that will enhance your sense of self
- Stand up for yourself—develop assertiveness skills and learn to work through conflict.
- Articulate the value of diversity and inclusion in decision making and power.
- Observe role models and mentors—observe skills and strengths of others and decide whether you wish to cultivate those as well.
- Engage in self-care—have a healthy and well-balanced lifestyle.
- Use your frustration and anger to empower your life—translate frustration and anger to energy to create change in the situations around you.
- Understand why you have chosen to rein yourself in, if you have—identify and acknowledge these situations and move on.
- Identify to what extent the values of modesty, reserve, and humility serve as barriers or strengths for you.

■ Engage in activism—develop alliances with power structures and set up policies and structures to make a difference.

■ Support and connect with each other—empowering others can be the same as empowering yourself.

■ Cultivate qualities of care, compassion, and kindness—be a supportive person.

Note. From "If Only I Knew Then What I Know Now: Perspectives of a Woman of Color," by M. J. T. Vasquez and C. J. Reyes, 2004, *Eye on Psi Chi, 8*(3), pp. 18–19, 33–35. Copyright 2004 by Psi Chi. Adapted with permission.

As never before, people are traversing the globe and bringing new ideas, customs, and ways of life into their homes. The advent of the Internet has transformed neighborhoods into a global society. These changes have set the stage for the transformation of psychology into a multicultural discipline (Vasquez et al., 2006). As a psychology major, you will have the opportunity to engage in growth-promoting activities that will enhance your ability to communicate and work effectively with people from cultures very different from your own. Achieving multicultural awareness and competency is a lifelong journey through exploration and discovery. Won't you come along?

Suggested Web Site

■ Psychology and Education Career Guidebook Series for Students of Color. This Web site provides guidebooks for high school and college students of color, including guidebooks for college students of color applying to graduate school and professional programs. See http://www.apa.org/pi/oema/careers/

Suggested Reading

American Psychological Association. (2003). Guidelines on multicultural education, training, research, practice, and organizational change for psychologists. *American Psychologist, 5,* 377–402.

Okun, B. F., Fried, J., & Okun, M. L. (1999). *Understanding diversity: A learning-as-practice primer.* Pacific Grove, CA: Brooks/Cole.

Ponterotto, J. G., Casas, J. M., Suzuki, L. A., & Alexander, C. M. (Eds.). (2001). *Handbook of multicultural counseling* (2nd ed.). Thousand Oaks, CA: Sage.

Vasquez, M. J. T., & Reyes, C. J. (Spring, 2004). If only I knew then what I know now: Perspectives of a woman of color. *Eye on Psi Chi, 8,* 18–19, 33–35.

Life After College: The World of Work for Psychology Majors 8

Most people who graduate with an undergraduate degree in psychology do not go to graduate school. That means that the majority of psychology majors use their talents and skills in a range of employment settings. This chapter focuses on discovering the breadth of occupational opportunities available to graduates with a bachelor's degree in psychology. It also focuses on learning how to present your psychology major as an asset by highlighting essential transferable skills and interests. The qualifications for many occupations more frequently include individuals with specific skill sets, interests, and work values than they do individuals with a specific college major. Instead, occupations typically require a college-educated individual who can communicate effectively, solve problems, learn new information quickly, and work well on a team. Refer to chapter 2 of this volume for a review of the many transferable skills developed by psychology majors.

Those with undergraduate degrees in psychology are particularly well suited for jobs involving helping people. Therefore, it will be no surprise that a number of job opportunities reside in the human services field. However, a diverse range of interests draw people to psychology, so you will learn that many people seek and find jobs in areas that you might not initially think are related to psychology. For example, this chapter includes an exploration of alternative career paths requiring graduate or professional training in areas outside of psychology, such as business, law, and public affairs or public administration. The following sections include a sample of occupations pursued by many psychology majors. Remember, this list is only a sample of occupations, representing some but not all of the jobs that you might consider. Use the descriptions that follow as a springboard for exploration of further opportunities. The descriptions include information culled from the *Occupational Outlook Handbook*, which is published by the U.S. Bureau of Labor Statistics and updated every 2 years, and O*NET, both excellent sources of occupational information. The *Occupational Outlook Handbook* is available online (see http://www.bls.gov/oco/home.htm). O*NET also is an online source of continuously updated occupational information (such as job descriptions, education and training requirements, and salaries), and it also includes interactive tools for exploring and searching for occupations and valuable assessments for people looking to find or change careers. O*NET is available online (see http://www.onetcenter.org/).

Nauta (2002) provided an outline of the particular types of occupational information that is useful to have as you explore your future possibilities. Perhaps most obvious is information about what the job or career entails, including typical job duties or work tasks. It also is helpful to know about other similar or related occupations. Find out about the potential salary range, minimum qualifications for various occupations, including the minimum and preferred level of education, licensing or certification requirements, which college majors are most preferred, and any specific physical requirements or desirable personality traits (e.g., outgoing, energetic). The job outlook is helpful information to help you plan for the future. For example, find out about opportunities for advancement and the turnover rate for employees. Lifestyle issues are important considerations in a job search. Consider the number of hours per week that you would be expected to work, whether weekend or evening hours, and/or travel are required. Would you be required to relocate? Remember to tap several sources for occupational information. Compare occupational descriptions in reference materials (e.g., *Occupational Outlook Handbook*) with people's firsthand experiences from working in the field.

Human Services

SOCIAL AND HUMAN SERVICES ASSISTANTS

A number of job titles are consistent with this type of occupation, including *caseworker, case manager, community support worker, mental health aide, community outreach worker, independent living specialist, activities of daily living specialist,* and *family development specialist.* Social and human services assistants provide direct and indirect client services to ensure that individuals maintain their maximum level of functioning. They assess client and family needs; establish their eligibility for benefits and services, such as food stamps, Medicaid, and welfare; and help them to obtain them. Other tasks include providing social, emotional, and family support; making appropriate referrals; making home visits; overseeing daily activities of people in residential placements; transporting clients to appointments and shopping; maintaining written records and reports; reporting progress to supervisors; assisting clients with money management, meal planning, and food preparation; and assisting those in need of supervision with personal hygiene and activities of daily living. They also support clients' participation in their treatment plans and communicate with all involved professionals. Some social and human services assistants work in offices, clinics, and hospitals, whereas others work in group homes, shelters, sheltered workshops, and day treatment programs.

Employers typically seek individuals who have a strong desire to help others, effective communication skills, a strong sense of responsibility, good time-management skills, patience, and understanding. The job outlook is good. The need for social and human services assistants is projected to grow much faster than the average for all occupations through 2014. Growth in this occupation will be spurred by the growing elderly population. In addition, more people will be needed to provide services to pregnant teenagers, the homeless, people with mental disabilities and those who are developmentally challenged, and substance abusers. Median annual earnings of social and human services assistants were $24,270 in 2004. The middle 50% earned between $19,220 and $30,900, the top 10% earned more than $39,620, and the lowest 10% earned less than $15,480.

PSYCHIATRIC AIDES

Specific job titles vary for this occupation. A sample of these titles includes *residential counselor, mental health worker, mental health technician,* and *psychiatric nursing aide*. Psychiatric aides assist mentally impaired or emotionally disturbed patients by working under the direction of a team that may include psychiatrists, psychologists, psychiatric nurses, social workers, and therapists. Typical tasks include organizing, supervising, and encouraging patient participation in social, educational, and recreational activities; observing patients and reporting any physical or behavioral signs that might be important for the professional staff to know; serving meals; and assisting patients with eating and grooming. Around 54% of all psychiatric aides work in hospitals, primarily in psychiatric and substance abuse hospitals. Some also work in psychiatric units of general medical and surgical hospitals. Other individuals are employed in state government agencies; residential mental retardation, mental health, and substance abuse facilities; outpatient care centers; and nursing care facilities.

Employers are interested in hiring individuals who have a desire to help others, are able to work as part of a team, have good communication skills, are tactful, patient, understanding, emotionally stable, and dependable. Psychiatric aides need to demonstrate skills in social perceptiveness and to be able to recognize when something is going wrong or is about to go wrong. They also need to have the ability to reason and think critically so that they can identify alternative solutions to problems. The job outlook for psychiatric aides is expected to grow more slowly than average for all occupations. Most job growth will be in residential mental health facilities and home health-care agencies. Demand for psychiatric aides in residential facilities will rise in response to growth in the number of older persons. Job growth could be affected by changes in government funding for programs serving those with mental illness. Median hourly earnings of psychiatric aides were $11.19 in 2004. The middle 50% earned between $9.09 and $14.09 an hour, the lowest 10% earned less than $7.63, and the highest 10% earned more than $16.74 an hour.

Health Care

MEDICAL AND HEALTH SERVICES MANAGERS

A number of job titles are consistent with this occupation including *office manager, health and social service manager, program manager, medical records manager, mental health program manager, nutrition services manager*, and *health information manager*. Entry level positions are typically administrative assistants or assistant department heads. Managers in all settings work to improve the quality and efficiency of health care while controlling costs. They establish objectives and evaluative criteria for the units they manage; develop and maintain computerized record management systems to store and process data and produce reports; ensure data security as required by law; establish work schedules and assignments for staff; maintain communication between governing boards, medical staff, and department heads; and keep informed of advances in data processing technology, government regulations, health insurance changes, and financing options. About 30% of the people employed in this occupation work in private hospitals; another 16% work in offices of physicians or in nursing care facilities. The remainder of people working in this occupation work in home health-care services, federal government health-care facilities, ambulatory facilities run by state and local governments, outpatient care centers, and community care facilities for the elderly. They also are employed by insurance carriers and health-care management companies that provide managed-care contract negotiations, physician recruiting, and management services to hospitals and other organizations.

Employers seek individuals who have good organization and managements skills, are skilled at data analysis, good communicators, exercise good judgment and decision making, can think critically to identify the benefits and deficits of alternative solutions, have good numeric and computer skills, and have good interpersonal skills. Employment of medical and health services managers is expected to grow faster than average for all occupations through 2014. Job opportunities will be especially good in offices of health practitioners, general medical and surgical hospitals, home health-care services, and outpatient care centers. The median annual earnings of medical and health services managers were $67,430 in 2004. The middle 50% earned between $52,530 and $88,210, the lowest 10% earned less than $41,450, and the highest 10% earned more than $117,990.

HEALTH EDUCATORS

Health educators sometimes have the job title *instructional coordinator*, *health promotion specialist*, *family educator*, or *wellness specialist*. Health educators collect and analyze data to identify community needs prior to planning, implementing, monitoring, and evaluating education programs designed to increase awareness and knowledge of healthy lifestyles, policies, and environments. Health educators often collaborate with health specialists and civic groups to determine the availability of services; design and implement training workshops, conferences, and school or community presentations; prepare and distribute health education materials; and provide public information including press releases, media campaigns, and program-related Web sites. People in these occupations need to stay up to date on changes in health-care technology to keep health education program material current. Many health educators work in hospitals and other health-care organizations and physician practices, nursing homes, community health agencies, and other community agencies and organizations.

Employers seek individuals who have a good knowledge of human behavior and performance, learning and motivation, principles and methods for curriculum design, teaching and instruction, and the measurement of training effectiveness. Good skills in verbal and written communication, persuasion and motivation, interpersonal relationships, and complex problem solving are typically required. The job outlook is expected to grow faster than average for all occupations through 2014. The median salary for health educators is $55,920.

Business

HUMAN RESOURCES MANAGERS

Human resources managers go by other job titles as well, including *director of human resources*, *human resources director*, *employee benefits manager*, and *employee relations manager*. Human resources managers plan, direct, and coordinate human resource activities of an organization and are responsible for recruitment, personnel policies, and regulatory compliance. They are responsible for administering compensation, benefits, and performance management systems and safety and recreational programs. To enhance morale and productivity, limit job turnover, and help organizations increase performance and improve business results, human resource managers also help their organizations effectively use employee skills, provide training and development opportunities to improve those skills, and increase employees' satisfaction with their jobs and working conditions. Human resources managers are often called on to assist in resolving work-related conflicts, particularly those between management and employees. They also must keep informed about equal employment opportunity and affirmative action guidelines and laws, such as the Americans With Disabilities Act. Most human resources managers work in an office of the organization that has employed them. Some of these managers are engaged in recruitment, which requires travel to attend professional meetings and visit college campuses to interview prospective employees.

Employers seek individuals who have good negotiation skills and are able to bring people together to reconcile differences and disputes. They also are interested in individuals who are good listeners and communicators. Given the growing diversity of the workforce, human resources managers must be sensitive and respectful of people with various cultural backgrounds, levels of education, and experience. They must be able to cope with conflicting points of view; function under pressure; and demonstrate discretion, integrity, and fair-mindedness. All of these sought-after skills make psychology majors good candidates for these positions. Some individuals decide to pursue a master's degree in human resource management to further their advancement in the field. Although the job outlook is good and is expected to grow faster than the average for all occupations through 2014, there will be stiff competition for jobs given the number of qualified college graduates. Median expected earnings vary by level of employment. In 2004, median earnings for the following positions were (a) employment, recruitment, and placement specialists: $41,190; (b) compensation, benefits, and job analysis specialists: $47,490; (c) compensation and benefits managers: $66,530; (d) training and development managers: $67,460; and (e) all other human resources managers: $81,810.

ADVERTISING AND PROMOTIONS MANAGERS

Advertising and promotions managers have other related titles, including *advertising director, marketing director, advertising sales manager*, and *ac-*

count executive. Advertising and promotions managers plan and direct advertising policies and programs and prepare budgets and estimates for costs for advertising campaigns. They also coordinate the market research, marketing strategy, sales, advertising, promotion, pricing, product development, and public relations activities. This involves coordinating activities of departments such as sales, graphic arts, media, finance, and research. Advertising and promotions managers also confer with clients to provide marketing and technical advice. Travel is sometimes required to meet with clients or representatives of communications media.

Employers seek mature, creative, and highly motivated individuals who handle stress well and are flexible and decisive. The ability to communicate persuasively with other managers, staff, and the public is vital. These managers also need tact, good judgment, and an exceptional ability to establish and maintain effective personal relationships with supervisory and professional staff members and clients. Psychology majors have the interpersonal knowledge and skill to be good communicators in these situations. Many people in these occupations begin at a lower level position and are promoted. Although experience, ability, and leadership are emphasized for promotion, participation in management training programs or continuing education opportunities can make someone a better candidate for promotion. Some people choose to get a master's degree in business administration (MBA) or marketing. The job outlook is good because jobs are expected to increase faster than average for all occupations through 2014. Although projected growth varies by industry, intense domestic and global competition for products and services will stimulate growth in this occupation. Median annual earnings in 2004 were $63,610 for advertising and promotions managers. Salaries vary substantially depending on the level of managerial responsibility, length of service, education, size of firm, location, and industry. For example, manufacturing firms usually pay managers higher salaries than do nonmanufacturing firms. In addition, many managers earn up to a 10% yearly bonus.

TRAINING AND DEVELOPMENT SPECIALISTS

Training and development specialists have a number of job titles, including *training specialist, training manager, corporate trainer, job training specialist,* and *management development specialist.* Training and development specialists conduct and supervise training and development programs for employees. They identify and assess training needs, help employees maintain or improve job skills, evaluate training materials and activities, and evaluate training effectiveness. By helping employees improve their skills, they effectively enhance productivity and work quality to achieve business results. Training and development specialists also help supervisors improve their interpersonal skills so they can deal effectively with employees. Some training specialists set up leadership or executive development programs among employees in lower level positions. Trainers assist new and existing employees with job transitions that result from mergers and acquisitions and technological changes.

Employers seek individuals with transferable skills in communication and the ability to select and use appropriate training and instructional materials and procedures when teaching new skills. Job candidates also need to demonstrate the ability to identify the educational needs of others, to create formal education and training programs, and to be able to develop productive interpersonal relationships with others. Psychology majors have these sought-after transferable skills in communication, assessment, and interpersonal relationships. The job outlook is expected to grow faster than the average for all occupations through 2014. Median annual earnings of training and development specialists were $44,570 in 2004. The middle 50% earned between $33,530 and $58,750, the lowest 10% earned less than $25,800, and the highest 10% earned more than $74,650.

College and University Student Affairs: Educational Administrators

Educational administrators typically advance through promotion from lower level positions to more responsible administrative positions. Educational administrators are often promoted from related staff jobs such as recruiter, residence hall director, financial aid or admissions counselor, or related positions in career services, residential life, student activities, and the alumni office. Because of the diversity of duties and levels of responsibility, job tasks vary considerably. Consequently, I offer a brief overview of several positions. *Registrars* are the custodians of students' records. They register students, record grades, prepare student transcripts, evaluate academic records, assess and collect tuition and fees, plan and implement commencement, oversee the preparation of college catalogues and schedules of classes, and analyze enrollment and demographic statistics. *Directors of admissions* manage the process of recruiting, evaluating, and admitting students. *Financial aid directors* oversee scholarship, fellowship, and loan programs.

Employers look for leadership, determination, confidence, innovativeness, and motivation. They also look for individuals who are good decision makers, have strong interpersonal skills, and are effective communicators. Knowledge of leadership principles and practices gained through work experience and formal education is important. Job outlook is good, and jobs are expected to grow as fast as the average for all occupations through 2014. Salaries vary greatly based on education, level of employment, and years of service. In 2004, the median salary for director of financial aid was $63,130, registrar was $61,953, and director of student activities was $45,636. Salaries for entry level positions are substantially less. To advance in this area, many people go on to earn a master's or doctoral degree in higher education administration.

Education

PRESCHOOL TEACHERS

The most typical job title is *preschool teacher*, however, other titles such as *prekindergarten teacher* and *early childhood teacher* also are used. Preschool teachers provide a variety of materials and resources for children to explore, manipulate, and use in learning activities and imaginative play. They use small-group lessons; one-on-one instruction; and learning through creative activities such as art, dance, and music to teach preschool children. Preschool teachers use children's play to further language and vocabulary development (e.g., using storytelling, rhyming games, and acting games), improve social skills (e.g., children working together to build a neighborhood in a sandbox), and introduce scientific and mathematical concepts (e.g., showing the children how to balance and count blocks when building a bridge). They are responsible for observing and evaluating children's performance, behavior, and social development—and discussing this with supervisors, parents or guardians, and child development specialists. They also attend to children's basic needs by assisting with feeding, dressing, and changing diapers. Preschool teachers work in public and private schools. Some private schools are associated with religious institutions. Many preschool teachers work year-round, but some do not work in the summer. Licensing requirements for preschool teachers vary by state. Requirements for public preschool teachers are generally more stringent than those for private preschool teachers. Private schools are generally exempt from meeting state licensing standards.

Employers seek individuals who are skilled at identifying the educational and developmental needs of children, developing formal educational programming, and teaching and instructing others. Preschool teachers have to be good communicators, skilled in classroom management, and be able to set and maintain consistent routines and expectations.

Jobs for preschool teachers are expected to grow much faster than the average for all occupations through 2014. Some states are instituting programs to improve early childhood education, such as offering full-day kindergarten and universal preschool. These programs, together with a projected higher enrollment growth for preschool age children, will create many new jobs for preschool teachers. The median annual wage in 2005 was $21,990.

TEACHER ASSISTANTS

Teacher assistants also are called *instructional assistants* or *teacher aides*. Some teacher assistants work with regular education students, but others provide extra help to special needs students, such as those with physical, learning, or emotional disabilities. They frequently provide tutoring and assist children either individually or in small groups to help them master learning material presented by the teacher. At times they supervise students in classrooms, hallways, cafeterias, school yards, and on field trips and perform clerical duties such as organizing and preparing lesson materials. Both public and private schools, preschool through 12th grade, employ teacher assistants.

Schools look for individuals who can communicate well with students, teachers, and parents or guardians. Teacher assistants should have the organizational skills required to coordinate, supervise, and manage students and be able to handle classroom situations with fairness and patience. Teacher assistants also must work well with teachers and demonstrate a willingness to follow their directions. Employment of teacher assistants is expected to grow about as fast as the average for all occupations through 2014. Median annual earnings of teacher assistants in 2004 were $19,410. The middle 50% earned between $15,410 and $24,320, the lowest 10% earned less than $13,010, and the highest 10% earned more than $29,220.

Law Enforcement: Probation Officers and Correctional Treatment Specialists

These occupations go by several job titles including *probation officer, community supervision officer, correctional counselor, parole agent, parole officer, correctional casework specialist, correctional probation officer, juvenile correctional officer*, and *probation counselor*. People in these occupations provide social services to assist in rehabilitation of law offenders in custody or on probation or parole. They are frequently required to make recommendations for actions involving the offender's treatment plan, conditional release, and education and employment stipulations. Other job tasks include preparing and maintaining case folders; writing progress reports; serving as a liaison with other agencies; and arranging for postrelease services such as employment, housing, counseling, education, and social activities. In the course of supervising offenders, probation officers and correctional treatment specialists may interact with individuals who are dangerous, angry, upset, or otherwise difficult to work with. Although the high stress levels can make these jobs extremely challenging at times, this work also can be rewarding. Many in this field obtain personal satisfaction from helping members of their community become productive citizens. Probation officers spend much of their time working for the courts. Correctional treatment specialists work in jails, prisons, or parole or probation agencies. In addition, extensive fieldwork may be required to meet with offenders who are on probation or parole.

Employers seek individuals, such as psychology majors, who have transferable skills in verbal and written communication, social perceptiveness, judgment and decision making, critical thinking, conflict resolution, problem solving, and negotiating as well as skills in organizing, planning, and prioritizing work. These jobs also require individuals to be able to maintain their composure and keep their emotions in check in difficult situations. Employment growth is projected to be about as fast as average for all occupations through 2014, depending on government funding. Median annual earnings of probation officers and correctional treatment specialists in 2004 were $39,600. The middle 50% earned between $31,500 and $52,100, the lowest 10% earned less than $26,310, and the highest 10% earned more than $66,660. In 2004, median annual earnings for probation officers and correctional treatment specialists employed in state government were $39,810; those employed in local government earned $40,560. Higher wages also tend to be found in urban areas.

Alternative Professional Career Paths Requiring Graduate and Professional Training

BUSINESS

Many psychology majors are good communicators, persuasive, interpersonally sensitive, and strong leaders. Therefore, some psychology majors may decide that further education in business is right for them. If you decide that a career in business is for you, and you want to obtain a graduate degree in business, you have a number of options. Most business schools offer a number of master's degrees based on area of specialization. The most common master's degrees awarded in business include accountancy, and general MBAs as well as specialist MBAs in health-care administration, computer and information science, labor relations and human resources, and public health. There also are a number of joint MBA programs, including joint nursing–MBA (MSN/MBA) and law–MBA programs (JD/MBA).

You may be wondering what it takes to get in. Most people pursuing an MBA have a bachelor's degree in any of a number of nonbusiness areas such as the humanities, social sciences (including psychology), engineering, and the sciences. Graduate programs in business vary in requiring, or recommending, a predetermined amount of work experience. Therefore, your work history is an important consideration in determining your admission into a graduate program in business. Schools vary as to the weight given to work experience, and admission officers recognize that the skills developed through employment also can be obtained in other ways such as extracurricular and community activities. When applicants do not have work experience or community or extracurricular activities, some schools will offer deferred admission, wherein the applicant is guaranteed acceptance into the MBA program after gaining a specified amount of experience. Applicants must take the Graduate Management Admissions Test (GMAT) for admission to almost all programs. The GMAT consists of three main parts, the Analytical Writing Assessment, the Quantitative section, and the Verbal section. GMAT scores are one measure of your potential for academic success in a graduate business program.

There is no standard curriculum for business schools; however, most schools expose students to a common body of knowledge in basic accounting, economics, finance, human resources and organization design, marketing, operations, policy, and quantitative methods and statistics. A growing number of MBA programs offer special programs and courses for those interested in improving the management of government and nonprofit organizations. For example, if you are interested in developing a multisite homeless shelter program, assessing the competitive position of a training program for displaced homemakers, administering a loan fund to support an urban housing development, or creating a market for municipal recyclables to support social service programs, then an MBA might be the degree for you. For more information on MBAs, see the career-related Web site maintained by the University of California, Berkeley (http://career.berkeley.edu/Grad/faqBusGrad.stm).

LAW

Psychology majors develop a number of skills easily transferable to the law profession. Becoming a lawyer requires a commitment to the ideals of justice and public service. Many people who become lawyers have a passion for argument and enjoy engaging in debate and discussion. One must have the ability to perform well at an academically rigorous level, think critically, synthesize material related to multifaceted issues, persuade and negotiate effectively, and write well. Lawyers advocate for the views of individuals and diverse interest groups and play a number of other roles, including counselor, interviewer, defender, proponent, and negotiator. These are just a few of the transferable skills that psychology majors bring to this profession. There are many subfields of law such as antitrust, civil rights, consumer protection, criminal, education, environmental, family, securities, and workers' compensation, to name just a few. The majority of lawyers (73%) work in private practice in small one-person offices or large firms. About 10% are employed by private industries and associations as salaried lawyers or managers, 8% work for government agencies, 1% work for legal aid or as public defenders, and 1% are involved in legal education. For more information, see the Web site of the Law School Admission Council (http://www.lsac.org).

The American Bar Association (ABA) does not recommend any particular college major but does suggest that students have a good knowledge of American history, political thought, economics, ethical theory and theories of justice, and math—as well as a basic understanding of human behavior and social interaction and the interaction between cultures and communities at home and abroad. For more information, see the ABA Web site (http://www.abanet.org/).

The Law School Admission Test (LSAT), administered by the Law School Admission Council (LSAC), is a half-day standardized test required for admission to all ABA-approved law schools, most Canadian law schools, and many non-ABA-approved law schools. Law schools use this test, which measures aptitudes important for legal thinking, as one of several factors in assessing applicants. It provides a standard measure of acquired reading and verbal reasoning skills. For a more complete description of the LSAT, visit the LSAC Web site (http://www.lsac.org). For resources on LSAT preparation and law school admission, see the suggested Web site links and readings at the end of this chapter.

Most law schools require 3 years of full-time or 4 years of part-time study. Law schools rely on the case method approach to teaching. First-year courses typically include civil procedure, constitutional law, contracts, criminal law and criminal procedure, legal method, legal writing and research, property law, and torts (LSAC, 2006).

PUBLIC AFFAIRS AND PUBLIC ADMINISTRATION

If you have an interest in applying your skills in decision making, problem solving, leadership, and organizing groups and would like to manage a government or nonprofit organization, then a master's degree in public affairs or public administration may be for you. The skills you will learn as a psychology major are good preparation for a career in leadership in public service. A master's degree in public affairs or public administration offers students flexibility in choosing what field they want to enter upon graduation. Graduates are found in a variety of fields and policy areas. As you work toward this degree, you will develop the skills needed by leaders and managers to implement policies, projects, and programs that resolve important societal problems and organizational challenges. You also can specialize in an area such as nonprofit management, health-care management, environmental management, criminal justice, and urban affairs. For further information, check out the Web site for the National Association of Schools of Public Affairs and Administration (NASPAA; http://www.naspaa.org/). The NASPAA Web site can be helpful in searching for a graduate school. Most graduate programs require that you take the Graduate Record Examination (GRE). For more information on the GRE, see chapter 9 of this volume and check out the GRE Web site (http://www.gre.org).

Those interested in working in the nonprofit sector should consult an excellent recent book entitled *Career Opportunities in the Nonprofit Sector*, by Jennifer Bobrow Burns (2006). In this book, Burns outlined positions across a broad range of nonprofits, including health and science; social service and religious organizations; advocacy and community development; arts and culture; colleges and universities; environment, nature, and conservation; and international jobs. The book also includes a complete bibliography and links to many useful Web sites.

The jobs that people get with a master's degree in public affairs or public administration vary greatly. This degree enables you to synthesize and transfer your college education, volunteer work, and professional experience into a career in an area of interest to you (e.g., health care, housing, human services). Salaries vary as well. In 2005, the median annual salary for someone working in the nonprofit sector was $49,500.

Preparing for a Job Search

You may now be wondering, "How and where do I begin my job search?" You may fear that you are about to enter unknown territory. The truth is, the best place to start is in your own backyard. Start with everyone and every place that is familiar to you. Searching for a new job, just like choosing a college or college major, can stir up some anxieties and fears. Why not initiate this pursuit in the company of supportive people in your life?

So now, the practical details. One of the best places to begin your job search is at your college or university's career counseling center. Career counseling centers typically host job fairs or post information about local job fairs. Most centers also provide numerous resources for writing resumes and cover letters (more on that later), databases for potential employers, job postings, and alumni networks. You also can ask your psychology department for a list of where their psychology alumni work. Although you might not personally know the alumni you contact, the shared history of attending the same school can create a climate of connectedness. Think about it: Have you ever run into someone who was from the same hometown as you or attended the same high school? Wasn't there a lot of energy and enthusiasm as you reminisced? Did you feel a sense of connection, however small? Having a point of connection is like having a foot in the door.

The next best place to turn is your existing network of family, friends, coworkers, current or previous supervisors, and college advisors. Be sure everyone you know is aware you are looking for a job and ask everyone if they know one or two people who could be good contacts for you. Having more eyes and ears on the lookout for potential opportunities can be a great benefit.

It is important to consult your local newspaper advertisements and the Internet for job listings. You also can explore local businesses and business directories for organizations in which you might be interested in working. Contact these organizations directly to learn more about them and to find out if they have any current or anticipated openings.

Applications, Resumes, and Cover Letters

What follows is a brief overview with tips for preparing these documents. For further information, you are encouraged to consult any of the numerous excellent sources of information and guidance for resume writing, job hunting, and interviewing. Some are listed at the end of this chapter.

Be sure to take the process of completing an application seriously. Your application communicates a lot about you to potential employers, telling them about your work habits, how well you follow instructions, your character, your personal achievements, your job performance, and your potential (Landrum & Davis, 2007). Carefully follow all of the instructions provided, be neat in completing the forms, and be completely accurate and honest in what you report. Also, it is a wise idea to let people know that you are listing them as references.

Your resume should answer two important questions for potential employers (Landrum & Davis, 2007): what you can do for them and why you should be considered for this job. It is important to accurately describe each of your work experiences, including your duties and responsibilities. Use action verbs to describe what you have accomplished. For a list of action words, consult the Quintessential Careers Web site (http:// www.quintcareers.com/action_verbs.html). Research has suggested that employers glance at a resume for 20 to 30 seconds (Krannich, 1991). Be succinct and to the point. Keep your resume to one or two pages. Neatness, spelling, and grammar count. Proofread your resume and have two other people proofread it for you.

There are two basic types of resumes: chronological and functional. A *chronological resume*, the most common, highlights the chronological progression of your educational and work history. There are several common sections in a chronological resume: a heading, objective, education, experiences, and activities and affiliations. The *heading* goes at the top of the resume and includes your name and all of your contact information. Remember to include contact information for your permanent residence, in addition to your campus address, if you will be moving at the end of the semester or returning back home for the summer. The *objective* is a concise statement of your goals and career focus. An example of an objective is, "To obtain an entry level position within a nonprofit organization requiring strong communication and analytical skills." The *education* section includes the institution awarding the degree, city, and state of the institution; name of the degree and the year it was awarded; college major and minor; academic honors; and the title of your senior research project if you completed one. In the *experience* section, all of your work experience (paid and unpaid, including part-time jobs, volunteer experiences, practical and internship experiences) is outlined, with your current or most recent job listed first. For each position, briefly describe your duties and responsibilities and specific skills and achievements. Include your job title and place and dates of employment. In the final section, *activities and affiliations*, list all professional affiliations, including student memberships in organizations such as the American Psychological Association, Psi Chi National Honor Society, and other groups. A sample chronological resume is provided in Exhibit 8.1.

A *functional resume* is organized around your strengths—meaning your skills, abilities, and accomplishments. The structure of a functional resume is to have a heading and an objective and then a separate section

EXHIBIT 8.1

Sample of a Chronological Resume

Susan Jones

Temporary Address:
Box 101
Huntington University
Collinwood, MA 12345
(555) 123-4567
susan.jones@huntington.edu

Permanent Address:
2424 Pleasant Street
Carsonville, MA 54321
(555) 123-7654
susan.jones@huntington.edu

OBJECTIVE To find a challenging position in a nonprofit organization utilizing communication and organizational skills.

EDUCATION Huntington University, Collinwood, MA. Bachelor of Arts in Psychology, May 2007. Minor: Business. Cum Laude Graduate. Senior Honor's Thesis: "Putting Student Services to Work Orienting College Freshmen"

EXPERIENCE *Peer Advisor*, Student Services Center. Huntington University, Collinwood, MA. September 2005–2006. Communicated with students to assist them in getting acclimated to campus life; encouraged student involvement in activities; created and presented workshops and programming.
Intern, Community Support Services. Smithtown, NY. Summer 2006. Supervised community volunteers; communicated with parents and guardians, staff, and supervisors; coordinated children's recreational programming; organized daily schedules.
Salesperson, Tower Department Store. Smithtown, NY. September 2002–May 2004.
Assisted customers in choosing products; organized merchandise; monitored and restocked inventory.

ACTIVITIES *Psychology Club Member*. September 2005–present. Organized club meetings; coordinated career fair; participated in fundraising events.

AFFILIATIONS *Student Affiliate Member*, American Psychological Association. September 2005–present.

REFERENCES Available on request.

for each set of skills and accomplishments in order of importance. Some students opt for a functional resume if their work and practical experiences are limited. A sample functional resume is provided in Exhibit 8.2. Refer to Exhibit 8.3 for basic tips on resume preparation.

The cover letter for your resume is arguably more important than the resume itself. Why is that? If you don't catch a potential employer's interest in the first few lines of your cover letter, it is less likely that he or she will bother to read the resume at all. If at all possible, address your

E X H I B I T   8 . 2

Sample of a Functional Resume

Susan Jones

Temporary Address:
Box 101
Huntington University
Collinwood, MA 12345
(555) 123-4567
susan.jones@huntington.edu

Permanent Address:
2424 Pleasant Street
Carsonville, MA 54321
(555) 123-7654
susan.jones@huntington.edu

OBJECTIVE To find a challenging position in a nonprofit organization utilizing communication and organizational skills.

COMMUNICATION EXPERIENCE
Peer Advisor, Student Services Center. Huntington University, Collinwood, MA. September 2005–2006. Communicated with students to assist them in getting acclimated to campus life; encouraged student involvement in activities; created and presented workshops and programming.

SUPERVISORY EXPERIENCE
Intern, Community Support Services. Smithtown, NY. Summer 2006.
Supervised community volunteers; communicated with parents and guardians, staff, and supervisors; coordinated children's recreational programming; organized daily schedules.

ORGANIZATIONAL EXPERIENCE
Psychology Club Member. September 2005–present. Organized club meetings; coordinated career fair, participated in fundraising events.
Salesperson, Tower Department Store. Smithtown, NY. September 2002–May 2004.
Assisted customers in choosing products; organized merchandise; monitored and restocked inventory.

AFFILIATIONS *Student Affiliate Member,* American Psychological Association. September 2005–present.

EDUCATION Huntington University, Collinwood, MA. Bachelor of Arts in Psychology, May 2007. Cum Laude Graduate.

REFERENCES Available on request.

letter to a specific person to avoid the use of a generic greeting such as, "To Whom It May Concern." Making an extra effort to find out not only to whom you should address the letter but also that person's exact job title demonstrates your conscientious effort, interest, and motivation. The first line of your letter should indicate which position you are applying for, and the bulk of your letter should highlight what you have to offer

EXHIBIT 8.3

Tips for Resume Preparation

Use standard size (8.5-inch × 11-inch) white or off-white paper.

Use a standard, nondecorative 12-point font.

Don't fold or staple your resume, and mail it in a large envelope.

If preparing an electronic resume, consult a Web resource for required formatting.

Have your resume reviewed and critiqued by a career counselor.

Communicate your strongest points first.

Use bullets, not lengthy sentences and descriptions.

Use the active, not passive, voice.

Use space to organize your resume (don't try to fit too many words into a small area; use blank lines for better visual appearance and balance).

Keep your resume current.

Note. From Landrum and Davis (2007, p. 45) and Kuther (2006, pp. 151–152).

the organization. The final portion of the letter should provide your contact information, thank the reader for his or her consideration, and provide a statement indicating your interest in their consideration and reply. A sample cover letter is provided in Exhibit 8.4.

Preparing for an Interview

You made it! You landed an interview! Now what? How do you put your best foot forward in an interview to make a great first impression? How should you dress? What should you do following the interview? There are a number of ways that you can prepare yourself to be at your best in a job interview. The most important thing to remember is to be yourself. You want to be hired for who you are. That's one of the best ways that both you and the employer will know whether you are a good match for the job and organization.

Before the interview, spend some time researching the organization that you are interviewing with. Find out as much as you can about the organization, its history and structure, and its goals and mission. Knowing as much as you can about an organization will be useful in your decision making and should help you feel a little more confident and comfortable walking into the interview. You will also impress the employer and demonstrate enthusiasm if you have spent time getting to know who they are and what they represent.

EXHIBIT 8.4

Sample Cover Letter

March 23, 2007

Ms. Maria Gonzalez
Director of Social Services
Family Focus
Collinwood, MA 12345

Dear Ms. Gonzalez,

I am writing to apply for the Program Assistant position at Family Focus that was advertised in *The Daily News* on March 16, 2007. I will complete my bachelor of arts degree in psychology in May 2007.

I have the organizational and interpersonal skills required to succeed in this position. My education and work experiences are good professional preparation for coordinating and delivering the programs offered by Family Focus. In addition, my responsibilities in the university's psychology club have helped to refine my skills in organizing and coordinating events and programs.

I have developed valuable skills working with children as an intern at Community Support Services. Therefore, I am very interested in learning more about your family services unit. I would like to meet with you to discuss my qualifications and the strengths that I could bring to your organization. I will contact you next week to discuss the possibility of scheduling a time that is convenient for you.

If you need any additional information, please contact me at 555-123-4567. I am enthusiastic about the possibility of working for your organization. I look forward to speaking with you.

Sincerely,

Susan Jones

Dressing appropriately for your interview is important. You want to look professional and demonstrate that you are taking this interview seriously. A good bet for men and women is a simple suit in a neutral color such as blue, gray, or black. A neat appearance is important. Jewelry should be kept to a minimum, and women are encouraged to go light on the makeup. You could carry a briefcase or portfolio with you to hold extra copies of your resume as well as any materials that the interviewer might give to you that day.

There are a number of other simple things that you can do. Blocher, Heppner, and Johnston (2001) have outlined a number of useful tips. Be on time or 10 or 15 minutes early. If you are early, this will give you some extra time to observe your surroundings and employee interactions. Bring a couple of extra copies of your resume. You may meet more than one person during your interview, and they all may not have had the opportunity to see your resume. Follow the interviewer's lead. Try not to control the interview or dwell too long on one point. Emphasize the positive, and never slight a former employer, colleague, or teacher. Even if you were challenged in these relationships, try to emphasize something positive. Never exaggerate or lie. It is better to be truthful than to embarrass yourself later. Emphasize what you can do for the organization. Reflect on your transferable skills and how you could use them in the organization's best interest. Be enthusiastic about the position and the organization. One way to demonstrate your enthusiasm is to show that you have done your homework and have learned about the organization. Wait for a job offer to bring up salary issues. It is always best to let the interviewer bring up salary. Finally, come prepared with questions to ask. Asking questions is one of the best ways to demonstrate your interest in a job and organization. Well-thought-out questions that also demonstrate knowledge of the organization are best.

What should you do when the interview is over? Send a thank-you letter immediately. Take this opportunity not only to thank the interviewer for his or her time but also to restate your interest in the position and how your skills are a good match for the organization's needs. Highlight something you learned about the organization during the interview that interested you or that you thought you could contribute to. Indicate when you will call the interviewer to follow up and then remember to do so. It also is important to keep in mind that interviewing is a learning process. Reflect on what made a particular interview go well and another not so well. Think about what you can do to change how you interview in the future on the basis of your past experiences.

Summary

As you can see, there are many realistic options that you can pursue with a bachelor's degree in psychology. The range of transferable skills that you will develop is broad enough to prepare you for diverse career paths. This chapter provides you with a brief exploration of the options and a few tips for preparing yourself for a job search. Have a look at the suggested Web sites and readings listed next for even more helpful information.

Suggested Web Sites

GENERAL OCCUPATIONAL INFORMATION

- O*NET: http://www.onetcenter.org
- Occupational Outlook Handbook: http://www.bls.gov/oco

JOB HUNTING

- Monster.com. This Web site is a place to post your resume, search for jobs, prepare for a job interview, and get other career advice: http://www.monster.com
- Union College Career Center: Resources and Handouts. This Web site provides information to help make students better prepared for career choices, constructing resumes, writing cover letters and thank you letters, interviewing, tips for navigating a career fair or networking event, and more: http://www.union.edu/Career/Info/Handouts/index.php

BUSINESS

- University of California, Berkeley: Career Development Center FAQs. This Web site provides answers to frequently asked questions about business school: http://career.berkeley.edu/Grad/faqBusGrad.stm
- The Association to Advance Collegiate Schools of Business. List of accredited colleges of business: http://www.aacsb.edu/
- Information about the GMAT: http://www.mba.com/mba

LAW

- American Bar Association (ABA). The ABA provides law school accreditation, continuing legal education, information about the law, programs to assist lawyers and judges in their work, and initiatives to improve the legal system for the public: http://www.abanet.org/
- American Bar Association Career Resource Center Online Pre-Law Toolkit. This Web site provides career information resources to individuals interested in a career in law: http://www.abanet.org/careercounsel/prelaw.html
- Law School Admission Council (LSAC). The LSAC is best known for administering the Law School Admission Test (LSAT®). Other useful information about law school also is provided on this Web site. See http://www.lsac.org/
- *Think About Law School.* This publication contains information that you need to know to begin preparing for and applying to law school: http://www.lsac.org/pdfs/2006-2007/ThinkAboutLawSchool2006.pdf

PUBLIC AFFAIRS AND PUBLIC ADMINISTRATION

- National Association of Schools of Public Affairs and Administration: http://www.naspaa.org/

- Association of University Programs in Health Administration. Information about undergraduate and graduate academic programs in the field: http://www.aupha.org
- Commission on Accreditation of Healthcare Management Education. Accredited graduate programs in medical and health services administration: http://www.cahmeweb.org
- American College of Healthcare Executives. Information about career opportunities in health-care management: http://www.healthmanagementcareers.org

Suggested Reading

JOB HUNTING

Blocher, D. H., Heppner, M., & Johnston, J. (2001). *Career planning for the 21st century* (2nd ed.). Denver, CO: Love.

Bolles, R. N. (2005). *What color is your parachute?* Berkeley, CA: Ten Speed Press.

Jansen, J. (2003). *I don't know what I want, but I know it's not this.* New York: Penguin Books.

Lore, N. (1998). *The pathfinder: How to choose or change your career for a lifetime of satisfaction and success.* New York: Simon & Schuster.

PSYCHOLOGY

DeGalan, J., & Lambert, S. (2006). *Great jobs for psychology majors.* Lincolnwood, IL: NTC/Contemporary.

Kuther, T. L., & Morgan, R. D. (2004). *Careers in psychology: Opportunities in a changing world.* Belmont, CA: Wadsworth.

O'Hara, S. (2005). *What can you do with a major in psychology?* Hoboken, NJ: Wiley.

BUSINESS

Kornegay, M. (2000). *Peterson's game plan for getting into business school.* Princeton, NJ: Peterson's.

Montauk, R. (2005). *How to get into the top MBA programs.* New York: Prentice Hall.

LAW SCHOOL

American Bar Association. (2003). *The official guide to ABA-approved law schools.* New York: Macmillan.

Ivey, A. (2005). *The Ivey guide to law school admissions: Straight advice on essays, resumes, interviews and more.* Orlando, FL: Harcourt.

Kaufman, D., Burnham, A., & Dowhan, C. (1998). *Essays that will get you into law school.* Hauppauge, NY: Barron's Educational Series.

Montauk, R. (2004). *How to get into the top law schools.* New York: Prentice Hall.

PUBLIC AFFAIRS AND PUBLIC ADMINISTRATION

Burns, J. B. (2006). *Career opportunities in the nonprofit sector.* New York: Ferguson.

Is Graduate School for Me? 9

Y ou may be wondering how relevant this chapter is for you, particularly if you are only just beginning to consider if an undergraduate major in psychology is right for you. If there is any chance that graduate school is in your future, the time for you to start thinking and planning for it is now. Yes, now, even if you are in your 1st or 2nd year of college. In fact, you are at the best point in your college career to consider this option. Now is the time that you can actually do something to improve your chances of getting into a graduate program. If you wait until your senior year of college, you may well be at a disadvantage compared with other students who have been enhancing their credentials over the past 3 years. This does not mean that if you are a senior or have already graduated all is lost. It is still possible to increase your chances of being admitted to a graduate program, although it may take some extra time and effort on your part. So either way, you cannot afford to put off reading this chapter.

In addition to ensuring that you have taken all of the required undergraduate psychology courses, there are many other things that you can do to make yourself a better candidate for graduate school. Applying to graduate school in psychology is extremely competitive. Some of the most competitive programs have acceptance rates of 20% or less (American Psychological Association [APA], 2007e). Good grades and good standardized test scores (e.g., Graduate Record Examination [GRE], Miller Analogies Test [MAT]) are important, but alone they are not enough. This chapter will help you to learn more about graduate study and explore the options that are available to you. Exploration and information gathering are the first steps toward deciding if a graduate degree in psychology is a desirable and attainable goal for you. All of life's decisions are made with some degree of ambiguity. We can never know with 100% certainty how our decisions will turn out. If we could, wouldn't life decisions be so much easier? Instead, we make the best choices we can with the information we have about ourselves and our options.

A good place to begin is to reflect on the reasons for pursuing a graduate degree in psychology and where that degree can take you. This chapter will guide you through exploring options for graduate study in psychology, strategies for graduate admissions success, important considerations about diversity, and how to narrow down your choices.

How Do I Know if Graduate School Is for Me?

Most people who pursue graduate study in psychology are highly committed and self-reliant individuals who express great interest in understanding human behavior, are invigorated by learning and the process of discovery, and possess great drive and ambition. Graduate school is not for everyone. You have to be ready to face rigorous academic demands that far exceed those faced in your undergraduate education. Graduate students who are the most satisfied and successful are those who possess an intellectual curiosity; like to read, do library research, and write papers; are interested in taking more methodology and statistics courses; are emotionally stable; and can effectively navigate multiple demands and responsibilities. The ability to manage one's time effectively and having a strong social support network also are big benefits.

WHAT ARE THE CAREER OPTIONS FOR SOMEONE WITH A DOCTORAL DEGREE IN PSYCHOLOGY?

In the United States, a doctorate is generally considered to be the entry level degree for the independent, licensed practice of psychology as a profession. The Association of State and Provincial Psychology Boards maintains a Web site (http://www.asppb.org) with links to state psychology boards for information about licensure in each particular state.

There are many reasons to pursue graduate study in psychology beyond the ability to practice in the profession. The doctoral degree provides the opportunity to specialize in a particular area or subfield of psychology, such as social, cognitive, or educational. It also offers broader career options, such as teaching and research opportunities at colleges and universities; higher average income; and more opportunities for clinical practice and supervision in a variety of public, private, and independent practice settings.

Many students pursue doctoral training because they are seeking a career in academia. Graduates of doctoral programs in psychology teach undergraduate, master's, and doctoral students in a variety of settings including community colleges, 4-year institutions, universities, professional schools of psychology, and medical schools. Remember that an academic position entails much more than just teaching. Professors also are involved in research and service to the university (e.g., advising, committee work, administrative responsibilities), community involvement (e.g., service projects and community support), and professional activities (e.g., membership and leadership roles in professional organizations). Other psychologists pursue research careers in universities, government, and private organizations (Kuther & Morgan, 2004).

Results of a survey of 2005 doctorate recipients in psychology indicated that the largest percentage of new graduates were employed in the human services sector (40%), followed by academia (30%); business, government, and other settings (19%); and schools and other educational settings (11%; Kohout & Wicherski, 2007). See the APA Center for Psychology Workforce Analysis and Research Web site (http://research.apa.org/) for a more detailed breakdown of employment settings. Many unique options are available to those with doctoral degrees in psychology, such as market research, business management, law, sports, textbook and education curriculum publishing, test publishing, and government and public policy work. See APA (2007b) for even more ideas on how others have used their doctoral degrees in psychology in interesting and nontraditional ways.

WHAT WOULD MY EARNING POTENTIAL BE WITH A DOCTORATE IN PSYCHOLOGY?

Median 1st-year annual salaries for 2005 ranged from approximately $44,091 for assistant professors and $50,000 for direct human services provided by clinical psychologists to approximately $74,500 for applied psychology positions in business or industry (Kohout & Wicherski, 2007). For additional up-to-date information on starting salaries for doctoral recipients in psychology, see the APA Center for Psychology Workforce Analysis and Research Web site.

The employment outlook for psychologists is good. Employment of psychologists is expected to grow faster than the average for all occupations through 2014 because of an increased demand for psychological services in schools, hospitals, social service agencies, mental health centers, substance abuse treatment clinics, consulting firms, and private companies. A particularly strong demand is anticipated for persons holding doctorates from leading universities in applied specialties such as clinical, counseling, and school psychology. Psychologists with extensive training in quantitative research methods and computer science will likely be the most sought after (U.S. Bureau of Labor Statistics, n.d.).

WHAT ARE THE COSTS ASSOCIATED WITH GRADUATE STUDY?

Doctoral study is not without its costs, both financial and otherwise. It requires a huge investment of time, energy, and money. Doctoral study also affects your lifestyle, including your social and family life. The demands and stresses, as well as the rewards, can be great. It typically takes 5 years to complete a doctoral degree. Annual tuition costs for psychology doctoral programs in state-run universities average over $11,000 per year for state residents, and $17,126 for nonstate residents (Kohout & Wicherski, 2007). Costs are generally higher for private institutions.

Graduate assistantships are frequently available to offset some of the costs to students. Students with graduate assistantships are typically required to work with a faculty member on research, teach a class or assist a faculty member in teaching a class, or perform some other service for the university. In return, most assistantships provide a tuition waiver and small stipend of approximately $11,000 (APA, 2007c). Fellowships and scholarships also are sometimes available. These sources of support typically do not require service to the department or university. The APA education Web site (http://www.apa.org/ed) is one resource for information about scholarships, fellowships, grants, and other funding opportunities.

As you can see, you need to give serious consideration to many factors before you embark on pursuit of a graduate degree. Have a look at Exhibit 9.1 for some good and bad reasons to pursue a doctoral degree.

DO I HAVE TO WRITE A DISSERTATION?

Most doctoral programs require you to write a *dissertation*, which is an original piece of empirical research done in partial fulfillment of the requirements of the doctoral degree program (Cone & Foster, 1993). A major purpose of the dissertation is to demonstrate the ability to conduct independent research that makes a contribution to knowledge on an important topic.

To complete a dissertation you will need the obvious skills of writing, methodology, and statistics, which you will begin to hone in your first semester of graduate work. Because psychology is a discipline based on empirical science, you will learn to understand and critique articles describing experiments (called *empirical* articles) and to design research projects

EXHIBIT 9.1

Good and Bad Reasons to Pursue a Doctorate in Psychology

Good reasons	Bad reasons
I have the drive and ambition to study psychology.	I'm afraid I won't get a job with a BA.
I want to expand my options for professional practice.	I want to be called "doctor."
I love research.	You don't have to go to a class while you write your dissertation.
I enjoyed my undergraduate methodology and statistics courses.	I hate math and just want to help people.
I like writing papers and doing library research.	I hope to work fewer hours for more pay.
My goal is to teach and conduct research.	I'd rather stay in school than get a job.
I would love to learn more about psychology.	I want the social status of having a doctorate.
I work well independently and manage my time effectively.	
I like to work with people.	
I like to help others.	

throughout your graduate program. So, although the dissertation may seem like a formidable task right now, by the time you reach this stage in your graduate education you will be prepared to undertake it.

Other requisite skills include good time-management and the ability to work well with others. You have to be able to effectively manage your time to complete this relatively long-term task. Good interpersonal skills will assist you in working effectively with your dissertation chairperson and other committee members. Don't go it alone. Develop your dissertation ideas in conjunction with a faculty member. Your dissertation should be part of an established program of research and in an area of expertise of your chairperson. No faculty member knows enough to supervise every dissertation topic, so it is essential to choose a topic related to faculty interest and expertise. Finally, be sure to nurture relationships that will offer you the support and encouragement you will need when the going gets tough (Cone & Foster, 1993).

Criteria for Admission: Do I Have What It Takes?

Admission requirements vary by program. Some requirements include specific coursework, a psychology major or minor, or a previous master's

TABLE 9.1

Minimum Required and Actual Scores of 1st-Year Doctoral Students, 2005–2006

Measure	Minimum required			Actual		
	M	*Mdn*	*N*	*M*	*Mdn*	*N*
GRE-V	521	500	93	574	575	254
GRE-Q	534	520	93	632	630	254
GRE-Analytic	4	5	10	5	5	29
GRE-Subject (Psychology)	553	550	30	645	650	98
Overall undergraduate GPA	3.10	3.00	213	3.55	3.58	244
Last 2 years GPA	3.22	3.00	89	3.68	3.70	92
Psychology GPA	3.25	3.00	75	3.79	3.70	64

Note. Data from American Psychological Association Center for Psychology Workforce Analysis and Research (2007). GRE-V = Graduate Record Exam, Verbal; GRE-Q = Graduate Record Exam, Quantitative Reasoning; GRE-Analytic = Graduate Record Exam, Analytical Writing; GRE-Subject = Graduate Record Exam, Subject; GPA = grade point average.

degree in psychology or a related field. Most universities have a required or suggested minimum grade point average (GPA) and/or test scores such as the GRE or MAT. Other criteria include research experience, volunteer or paid work experience in an area relevant to psychology, extracurricular activities, letters of recommendation, a personal statement, and an interview. Specific undergraduate courses (e.g., statistics, laboratory-based experimental courses) also may be required.

Applying to graduate school is much more involved and time-consuming than applying to undergraduate college. Depending on the programs that you apply to, the process can be a highly competitive one as well. How competitive? Well, have a look at Table 9.1 to get an idea of the minimum required GRE and GPA as well as the actual scores of students admitted to doctoral programs in psychology. These data were compiled by the APA Center for Psychology Workforce Analysis and Research from questionnaires sent to graduate departments and schools of psychology. As you can see, in most cases the actual scores of those admitted typically exceed minimum requirements. Acceptance and enrollment rates for doctoral programs vary by psychology subfield. As Table 9.2 shows, doctoral programs in social and personality psychology are the most competitive subfields for admission, followed by child and adolescent psychology (including child clinical), and health psychology. When requesting information from specific graduate programs, be sure to inquire about the number of applications received and accepted by each individual program to get an idea about how competitive each program is.

TABLE 9.2

Acceptance and Enrollment Rates for Doctoral Programs by Subfield, 2005–2006

Subfield of psychology	Acceptance rate			Enrollment rate		
	No. of programs	*M*	*Mdn*	No. of programs	*M*	*Mdn*
Experimental psychology (general and applied)	70	25.6	20.5	70	17.3	14.2
Developmental psychology	100	23.7	18.8	91	14.7	10.0
Social and personality psychology	98	13.1	1.0	88	0.8	0.5
Clinical psychology	234	20.6	10.0	216	13.9	0.7
Counseling psychology	68	19.6	15.2	64	14.2	10.4
School and educational psychology	93	40.8	37.0	86	31.1	21.7
Neuroscience/ physiological/ biological psychology	84	26.5	20.0	76	20.0	12.5
Industrial/organizational psychology	55	21.2	18.8	52	13.4	0.7
Cognitive psychology	96	28.2	24.8	91	16.7	14.3
Health psychology	18	18.5	1.0	18	10.1	0.8
Child and adolescent psychology (including child clinical)	23	16.0	10.5	22	11.3	0.8
Neuropsychology	11	20.7	17.9	6	13.2	11.8
Other	109	29.9	25.0	100	22.6	17.6
Not specified	4	21.5	13.6	4	11.5	13.6
Total	1,063	24.2	17.2	984	16.6	10.7

Note. From American Psychological Association Center for Psychology Workforce Analysis and Research (2007).

You might be wondering, "How important can GRE scores really be?" In a survey of graduate programs of psychology, APA (2007c) reported that program directors ranked personal statements of goals and objectives first in importance in admissions decisions, letters of recommendation were a close second, and GPA was ranked third. Test scores ranked sixth, just after research experience. So, although GRE scores were not ranked the highest, remember that you first have to get yourself in the running by meeting the minimum preferred or required scores. See Table 9.3 for the complete ranking of criteria used in graduate admissions decisions.

What else do graduate programs want? When all other factors are equal, a survey of faculty members involved in graduate admissions decisions identified the following factors as important criteria in evaluating applications: status and reputation of applicant's references; underrepresented ethnic minority group membership; number of statistics, re-

TABLE 9.3

Importance of Various Criteria in Admissions Decisions, 2005–2006

Criteria	M	SD	Mdn	N
GRE and MAT scores	2.52	0.56	3.00	381
Research experience	2.53	0.66	3.00	421
Work experience	1.86	0.67	2.00	412
Extracurricular activities	1.40	0.54	1.00	378
Clinically related public service	1.93	0.68	2.00	377
Grade point average	2.75	0.44	3.00	424
Letters of recommendation	2.83	0.42	3.00	425
Interview	2.65	0.59	3.00	367
Goals and objectives	2.85	0.38	3.00	427
Other criteria	2.83	0.38	3.00	52

Note. Ratings are based on the following coding scheme: 1 = low; 2 = medium; 3 = high. From American Psychological Association Center for Psychology Workforce Analysis and Research (2007). GRE = Graduate Record Examination; MAT = Miller Analogies Test.

search methodology, and advanced science courses taken; prestige of applicant's undergraduate institution; and honors or merit scholarships awarded by the undergraduate institution (Keith-Spiegel, Tabachnick, & Spiegel, 1994).

What Are the Options for Graduate Study in Psychology?

WHAT ABOUT EARNING A MASTER'S DEGREE?

So far, we have only discussed the option of doctoral study. It also is possible to pursue a master's degree in psychology. This is sometimes an option for people who are unsure that they want to commit to a doctoral program and for those who need some extra preparation for doctoral study. Most master's programs require coursework, supervised experience, a research thesis, and comprehensive exams. Some psychology departments also offer specialist degrees in a particular area, such as school psychology. Specialist degrees generally require an additional year of coursework and supervised experience beyond the master's degree. A specialist degree is a typical requirement in most states for certification to practice in the schools as a school psychologist. It is important to remember that many doctoral programs will accept few, if any, credits for master's level work from another program.

Those with a master's degree in psychology are employed in a variety of occupations. The highest percentage of people with this degree work in schools and other educational settings (25%); followed by business, government, or other settings; other human service settings; hospitals and clinics (each at 19%); and university and college settings (13%; Singleton, Tate, & Kohout, 2003). New master's degree recipients can expect to earn less than doctoral level psychologists. A 2002 survey of people who held master's degrees in psychology found that annual salaries ranged from $48,000 for those employed in applied psychology settings and $41,250 for direct human service positions in school psychology to $29,000 for clinical psychology degree recipients working in direct human services positions in community mental health centers (Singleton et al., 2003).

WHAT IS THE DIFFERENCE BETWEEN A PhD AND A PsyD?

The PhD degree is considered a research degree with an emphasis on research training and the integration of research with applied or practical training. It is the most frequently awarded degree in psychology: about 75% of all doctoral degrees in psychology are PhDs (APA, 2007d). The PsyD is a professional degree in psychology; PsyD programs place an emphasis on preparing graduates for professional practice. Typically, the focus is much less on research in these degree programs than in PhD programs. PsyD degrees are most frequently awarded in independent professional schools of psychology (APA, 2007d). The EdD is a third degree that is typically available in programs such as educational psychology and is housed in colleges or schools of education.

SUBFIELDS OF PSYCHOLOGY

When you apply to graduate school, you apply to a specific program or subfield within psychology. In general, there are two groups of subfields: applied subfields and those that prepare you for careers in academic and research settings. Applied subfields lead to professional practice in psychology and licensure as a psychologist. These subfields include clinical, counseling, school, and industrial/organizational psychology. Some subfields also provide the training required to become a health service provider. These include clinical neuropsychology, community psychology, geropsychology, and health psychology. The remainder of the subfields are generally research subfields and do not lead to traditionally based practice (e.g., assessment and psychotherapy). However, researchers in these fields may in fact engage in applied research in which the results of their work have practical applications to real world problems. Refer to

TABLE 9.4

New Doctorates in Psychology by Subfield, 2004–2005

Subfield	N	%
All subfields	5,074	100
Clinical psychology	2,450	48
School and educational psychology	430	8
Counseling psychology	416	8
Other	373	7
Developmental psychology	236	5
Experimental psychology (general and applied)	216	4
Social and personality psychology	210	4
Cognitive psychology	190	4
Industrial/organizational psychology	178	4
Child and adolescent psychology (including child clinical)	133	3
Neuroscience/ physiological/ biological psychology	113	2
Health psychology	87	2
Neuropsychology	42	1

Note. From American Psychological Association Center for Psychology Workforce Analysis and Research (2007).

chapter 1 of this volume for general descriptions of the major subfields of psychology. Also, have a look at Table 9.4 for the number of new doctorates in psychology by subfield. For more detailed information, refer to the suggested reading at the end of the chapter. You may need to do some real self-reflection to come to a decision about which subfield is right for you: Think about what you want to do with your knowledge in psychology and what kind of career you want in psychology.

ACCREDITATION STATUS

Some states require that you graduate from an APA-accredited doctoral program to meet the eligibility requirements for licensure as a psychologist. *Accreditation* is a system for recognizing educational quality as defined by the profession or other organizations. It involves a voluntary process of self-examination and external review to evaluate, enhance, and publicly recognize quality in institutions and programs of higher education. Accreditation is intended to protect the interests of students, benefit the public, and improve the quality of teaching, learning, research, and professional practice (APA, 2007a). The APA accredits applied psychology doctoral programs in clinical, counseling, school, and combined programs. Accreditation is not pertinent to other subfields. Accredited programs have met the minimum standards of training (i.e., coursework, qualified faculty, adequate field experiences) set forth by the APA Com-

TABLE 9.5

Common Theoretical Orientations

Theoretical orientation	Description
Psychodynamic	Based on the idea that thoughts and emotions are important causes of behavior and that observable behavior is a function of a person's deepest emotions and feelings.
Behavioral	Focused on learning as the basis of behavior and on the role of environmental rewards and punishments in altering behavior.
Cognitive	Emphasizes thoughts and how people acquire and interpret information and use it in solving problems.
Social–cognitive	Based on the idea that internalized beliefs, perceptions, and goals influence the impact that experiences associated with learning have on behavior and thoughts.
Humanistic	Emphasizes a human's striving towards self-actualization, or being all that a person can be.
Existentialism	Emphasizes self-determination, choice, and the responsibility of individuals to create the meanings of their life.
Community–cultural	Focuses on people's ability to cope effectively with stress and the role of one's social support system.

Note. Data from Sarason and Sarason (2002, pp. 61–80).

mittee on Accreditation. APA maintains current listings of accredited programs (APA, 2007a).

THEORETICAL ORIENTATION AND TRAINING MODEL

Graduate programs at different universities may have different theoretical orientations, such as humanistic, cognitive–behavioral, or psychodynamic. Review each program's materials carefully. Look closely at the emphasis in the program description, course offerings, and faculty interests. Many programs have faculty that represent a range of theoretical orientations, while others tend to specialize or focus on a particular orientation. It is important to know this before you apply so that you choose a program with an orientation that best matches your interests. See Table 9.5 for brief descriptions of some of the most common theoretical orientations.

Most graduate programs in psychology follow three broad training models: The *scientist–practitioner model*, the *practitioner model*, and the *re-*

searcher–scientist model. The most widely adhered to model of doctoral training for clinical, counseling, school, and industrial/organizational psychology is the scientist–practitioner model. This approach to training also is called the *Boulder model,* named after a conference held in Boulder, Colorado, in 1949. This conference formalized the training approach that gives equal weight to both research and practice. Programs adopting this model of training typically prepare their graduates to effectively integrate science with practice, thus preparing them for careers in both academia and practice. The practitioner model primarily trains students to provide psychological services, with less emphasis on science and research. Programs adhering to this model typically award the PsyD and prepare individuals to become full-time practitioners. This approach to training has alternatively been called the *Vail model,* named after a conference held in Vail, Colorado, in 1973. In programs that follow the researcher–scientist model, students receive training in their specific subfield content area as well as rigorous training in research methods and statistics. These programs typically train individuals for careers in teaching and research. Historically, this was the first training model for psychologists. This model is frequently found in graduate programs of psychology in experimental, social and personality, quantitative, physiological, and developmental psychology.

PRESTIGE AND NATIONAL RANKING OF THE PROGRAM

As with other fields, more prestigious programs are more sought after. For some psychology subfields, professional rankings are based on the research productivity of faculty members. These rankings can sometimes be found in articles in professional journals. Various reporting sources rank doctoral programs in psychology, including *U.S. News and World Report* and the National Research Council (NRC). *U.S. News and World Report* bases its rankings solely on the ratings of academic experts. To gather data, they ask deans, program directors, and senior faculty to judge the academic quality of programs in their field on a scale of 1 (*marginal*) to 5 (*outstanding*). (See U.S. News & World Report, 2007.)

Another group that ranks doctoral programs in psychology is the NRC, which provides an assessment of the quality and characteristics of research-doctorate programs in the United States. They collect information through questionnaires administered to institutions, programs, faculty, and advanced doctoral students (in selected fields) as well as information on publications, citations, and dissertation keywords. According to the NRC, rankings help universities improve the quality of programs through benchmarking and provide potential students and the public with accessible, readily available information on doctoral programs. Prestige of a program may be a factor that can be considered in job searches after completing your degree. For more information, visit the National Academies Web site (http://www7.nationalacademies.org/resdoc/index.html).

OTHER INDICATORS OF PROGRAM QUALITY

Other ways to assess the quality of a program include looking at the attrition rate of students. Find out how many incoming doctoral students actually complete their degree, how long it takes them to do so, and how quickly (and in which settings) graduates obtain work after completing the program. This information might be available on the department Web site, or you might be able to obtain it from the department chairperson. The average time to complete a doctoral degree is 5 years. It should be a matter of concern if most students in a program do not complete their degree in 5 years or less. Look closely at the program's available resources, such as computer labs, library facilities, and funding for travel to present at conferences or for costs associated with dissertation research. Finally, assess the availability of graduate assistantships to help finance your educational costs.

Strategies for Graduate Admissions Success

Gaining acceptance into a graduate program of psychology requires advance planning, first and foremost. Use your undergraduate years as a time to gain the experience and skills you need; explore the various subfields of psychology and options for graduate study; develop good relationships with professors to garner better letters of recommendation; prepare yourself financially and psychologically for the costs and demands of a graduate education; and explore your passions, interests, and plans for the future. Various psychologists have developed a number of suggested guidelines on how to prepare a "successful" graduate admissions application (e.g., APA, 2007c; Buskist, 2001; Keith-Spiegel & Wiederman, 2000; Lunneborg & Wilson, 1987). The following is an outline of the most frequently cited recommendations for preparing the best application that you can.

BE PLANFUL

Applying to graduate school in psychology can be a complex process involving research, preparation, and careful planning. You need to know what you want to do professionally, which schools have the best training programs to meet your needs and interests, and what the application process involves at each school. During your sophomore year and early in your junior year, you should start to narrow down your options for the specialization of psychology that you are interested in and begin to explore the best training programs in that subfield. You also should begin to consider which professors you will ask for letters of recommendation and what you will say about yourself in your *letter of intent*. A letter of intent is similar to a college admissions essay. Its purpose is to communicate your interests, skills, and aspirations in your field of interest. During your sophomore and junior year is also a good time to begin to review for the GRE so that you will be prepared to take it for the first time in the spring of your junior year. See Table 9.6 for a more complete timeline.

You need to decide how many programs that you will apply to. Applying to up to 10 programs is wise, particularly if the program specialization is a competitive one. One or 2 of these schools could be your "dream" choices, and the majority of the other programs could be ones that you think you have a good chance of being accepted into and would be a good match for your interests and goals. It never hurts to apply to 1 or 2 schools that have a slightly less competitive edge to improve your chances of getting accepted somewhere. Think of the application process as an investment, because it is an investment, not only in your time and money, but in your career and future earning potential. The average application fee for doctoral study is $56 (APA, 2007c). There also are expenses associated with taking standardized tests (e.g., GRE, MAT) and requesting official copies of your transcript. Application deadlines typically fall between January 15 and March 1 of each year. APA-accredited clinical and counseling psychology programs tend to have the earliest deadlines. The median deadline for these programs is January 15 (Norcross, Kohout, & Wicherski, 2006).

DEVELOP COMPETENCIES AS AN UNDERGRADUATE

Developing special strengths can mean the difference between being accepted or not when all of the other factors are equal. For example, if your grades and GRE scores are as high as those of other applicants, your specialized competencies and your ability to write about them in your letter of intent could mean the difference between acceptance and rejection. While an undergraduate, you should work on developing writing skills; statistical, methodological, and analytical skills; computer and technical skills; clinical skills; skills in teaching; and skills in a foreign language.

TABLE 9.6

Timeline for Graduate Admissions Tasks

Time	Tasks
Sophomore year	Begin to participate in as many psychology club activities as possible.
	Take one or more math, science, or computer science courses beyond those required.
	Get to know psychology faculty and make some initial contacts to talk about participating in research activities.
	Learn more about professional organizations and explore the possibility of attending a regional or state conference.
Junior year	Begin to participate in research activities with a faculty member.
	Get practical experience.
	Continue to develop good relationships with faculty and think about potential referees.
	Obtain information about the Graduate Record Examination (GRE) and preparation courses and materials.
	Learn about graduate programs and begin to consider which match your interests.
	Take the GRE in the spring.
Summer before senior year	Obtain more detailed program information from specific programs and faculty.
	Prepare your resume.
	Begin to narrow your choices of programs to apply to.
Senior year: September–October	Retake GRE or take it if you have not yet taken it.
	Make final decisions about where to apply.
Senior year: November	Request letters of recommendation from faculty.
	Write your letters of intent.
	Complete your resume.
	Request test scores and transcripts to be sent to all schools to which you are applying.
Senior year: December	Complete and submit all applications by required due dates.
	Apply for assistantships and other sources of support (e.g., scholarships, loans).
	Keep photocopies of all applications.
	Follow up with programs to be sure that your applications are complete before due date.

INVOLVE YOURSELF IN UNDERGRADUATE RESEARCH

Become involved in research as early as you can. The earlier you begin, the more likely it will be that your involvement will result in a professional presentation or publication. Research experience looks good on your resume, but a presentation or publication looks even better. You also will gain more confidence in the research process if you have the experience of doing a presentation. In addition, your strongest letters of recommendation will most likely come from professors with whom you have done research.

DO YOUR HOMEWORK ON POTENTIAL GRADUATE SCHOOLS

Finding the right match for your interests and qualifications can be a time-consuming venture, but it is time well spent. The best place to begin is to get a copy of APA's most recent edition of *Graduate Study in Psychology*, which provides information related to graduate programs of psychology in the United States and Canada. This book is an excellent resource that includes program descriptions, admissions requirements, average GPA and GRE scores of recently accepted students, and the availability of financial assistance. It is organized alphabetically by state and then by institution. Once you have identified a number of schools, you can take the next steps and get additional information from the universities themselves. Most university psychology department Web sites provide detailed program information including the focus of the program, course descriptions, information about the faculty, application procedures and timetable, and funding. Exhibit 9.2 provides an outline of important information that you should obtain for each program that you are seriously considering.

IDENTIFY POTENTIAL MAJOR PROFESSORS OR MENTORS

One of the best ways to choose schools that are the best matches for you is to find universities that have faculty members with interests that are similar to yours. In many cases, their vitae will be online, often with a list of publications that represent their scholarly interests. If this information is not readily available online, have your college or university reference librarian assist you in conducting a literature search to locate recent faculty publications. You might even want to contact faculty who have scholarly interests similar to yours, introduce yourself, and let them know

Graduate Program Questions

For each graduate program you are considering, research to find out answers to the following questions.

1. What is the profile of students recently admitted to the program with respect to academic background, GRE scores, and demographic characteristics?
2. What is the program's "track record" in students admitted who graduate and the average number of years required to achieve a degree?
3. What are the goals and objectives of the program and do they match my interests and capabilities as a graduate student?
4. For programs with an emphasis on academic and research careers, what is the record of graduates' success (during the first 5 years) in obtaining postdoctoral research fellowships, academic appointments, or applied research positions outside the academy?
5. For programs with an emphasis on professional practice, what is the program's accreditation status (if applicable), the record of its graduates' success in obtaining licensure, and its graduates' selection for advanced practice residencies and professional development in their first 5 years?
6. For programs that require an internship or practicum, what is the success rate of placement for students attending the program?
7. What financial resources are available to students, and what is the average level of indebtedness among recent graduates of the program?

Note. From American Psychological Association (APA; 2007d). Many of the questions posed can be researched through APA's Graduate Study in Psychology subscription Web site (http://www.apa.org/gradstudy/) as well as the individual program's Web site. If neither source yields the desired data, contact the program directly.

that you will be applying to their program. Getting your name recognized could help, particularly if you can talk knowledgeably with faculty about their research.

PREPARE FOR THE GRADUATE RECORD EXAMINATION OR MILLER ANALOGIES TEST

Graduate Record Examination Overview

The GRE is a standardized aptitude test that is thought to predict success in graduate school. GRE scores are typically a required part of your application for graduate admission. The GRE consists of two separate tests, the General Test and the Subject Test. The General Test measures critical thinking, analytical writing, verbal reasoning, and quantitative reasoning skills. It has three subtests: Verbal Reasoning, Quantitative Reasoning, and Analytical Writing.

The GRE Subject Test assesses achievement in eight specific fields of study to help predict one's potential for success in graduate school. Each Subject Test is intended for use with students who have majored in, or have an extensive background in, that particular subject area. The Psychology Subject Test is frequently required with graduate admissions applications. Questions on the Psychology Subject Test are drawn from the most commonly offered undergraduate psychology courses. The questions rely on factual information and the ability to analyze relationships, apply principles, draw conclusions from data, evaluate research designs, and/or identify psychologists who have made theoretical or research contributions to the field.

Graduate Record Examination Test Prep

To score well, it is recommended that you take time to prepare for the GRE by becoming familiar with the basic structure and content of the General and Subject Tests. There are many commercial study guides available for self-study, as well as test preparation courses. GRE makes available a number of free general test-preparation materials, including practice test software available free on the GRE Web site (http://www.gre.org). Sample test questions for the revised General Test also are available on the Educational Testing Service Web site (http://www.ets.org/gre). A good way to prepare for the Psychology Subject Test is to review a good undergraduate introductory psychology text, such as *Basic Psychology* (Gleitman, Fridlund, & Reisberg, 2003), or *Psychology: In Search of the Human Mind* (Sternberg, 2000).

Miller Analogies Test Overview

Only a few programs require the MAT, which is a 1-hour test of verbal reasoning and word association through word analogies. The test is available in both paper-and-pencil and computer versions, both administered by Harcourt Assessment. For more information on the test and practice materials, consult their Web site (http://www.milleranalogies. com).

WRITE AN OUTSTANDING LETTER OF INTENT

The letter of intent is your opportunity to personalize your application and market yourself. It is important to clearly articulate your interests in psychology, how specific educational and work experiences have helped you to build those interests, your aspirations and future professional goals, skills, personal strengths, why a career in psychology appeals to you, and what attracts you to each specific program. Be specific in describing your academic interests in psychology, particularly your interests in research. Whenever possible, link your current interests to your involvement in previous research. If your contributions to a research project resulted in professional presentations or publications, be sure to indicate this. Note whether the research you were involved in was completed as part of a course requirement, independent study, or extracurricular experience. Be specific in describing any relevant volunteer, internship, or paid work experiences you have had, and how these experiences have shaped your career goals. Mention your relevant personal and academic accomplishments that you are most proud of and any traits, work habits, and attitudes you possess that will likely contribute to your academic success in graduate school.

Your letter should be clear, concise, and well organized. Letters of intent are typically two to three single-spaced pages in length. Anything shorter will not provide enough detailed information. Letters that are too long are likely to be wordy and repetitive. Be succinct and attend carefully to spelling and grammar. Have someone (or several people) proofread your statement. Remember, it is not only what you say, but how you say it. Admissions committees also see your letter of intent, or personal statement, as a sample of your writing skills. Poorly written statements can hurt even the best applications.

Avoid writing a one-size-fits-all letter. Programs are most interested in admitting talented students who have interests, goals, and theoretical orientations that closely match those of the program and the faculty. This means that you have to do your homework on each program that you apply to. In your statement you must demonstrate that you have fully researched the program, are familiar with its curriculum and faculty, and have the abilities, skills, and interests that provide a good match to what the program has to offer. Use specific concrete examples when describing your experiences that have prepared you for graduate study and have led you to apply to each particular program. Discuss how the program that you are applying to can help you to achieve your goals. If there is a faculty member who has interests similar to yours, make that known in your statement. Do not be afraid to discuss your interest in the research of several faculty members because not all faculty will be looking for new students each year. The more you already know about faculty members' work and interests and the more you are able to intelligently communicate a genuine interest in working with them, the more likely that a good match will be identified by those making admissions decisions.

SECURE STRONG LETTERS OF RECOMMENDATION

Most programs require between three and four letters of recommendation. Typically, programs prefer these letters to come from someone who is familiar with your academic work. Therefore, professors who know you well should be at the top of your list when considering who to ask for letters of recommendation. Some programs may ask for a recommendation from people who have supervised your work in practical settings.

How you ask for recommendation letters also is important. Be sure to ask people in person if they are willing to serve as a reference for you. This gives you the opportunity to assess how willing and enthusiastic they are to serve as a reference for you. It also is a good idea to ask your potential references if they would feel comfortable writing you a good or strong letter of recommendation. If they seem hesitant or noncommittal, thank them and let them know that you will get back to them. If it turns out that you have plenty of people who would enthusiastically write you a good letter of recommendation, you may not need this person's letter after all. An in-person meeting also provides an opportunity for your potential references to ask you questions that might assist them in writing you a better letter. You also can use this opportunity to ask for advice and tips on preparing your application.

A good way to approach someone for a letter is to first let the person know why you selected him or her. You might try, "I thought you would be a good person to ask for a reference because you are familiar with my research skills [performance in class/leadership in the psychology club, etc.]." Be sure to begin asking potential references well in advance of your first application deadline. At least a month's notice is ideal.

To demonstrate your organizational ability and further highlight your experience and skills for those people who will ultimately write your letters of recommendation, gather all needed reference recommendations in one packet. Not only will that demonstrate your organizational skills, it also will help to ensure that nothing gets misplaced or forgotten. Provide each person writing you a reference with a table that lists every program that you would like letters of recommendation sent to, along with the specifics about the type of program (e.g., master's or doctoral degree and subfield), the date that the letter is due, and the address that it should be sent to. Arrange the table so that the program with the first due date is at the top of the list. Be sure all reference forms are filled out (typed) by you where appropriate and signed by you indicating if you are waiving your right to see the letter. It is advisable to waive your right to see the letter; confidential letters yield more trust in the content. Many faculty members will still provide you with a copy of the letter, anyway. Finally, provide stamped addressed (typed) envelopes for each of the letters.

Provide your references with an updated resume with your current contact information, all relevant research, volunteer and work experiences, awards and special accomplishments, and memberships in professional organizations (e.g., Psi Chi, APA). Be detailed in describing your research experiences (e.g., conducted literature searches, collected data, data entry), including any professional presentations or publications that you were involved in. It is often helpful to provide a transcript with all of the courses highlighted that you took from that professor. Be sure to include an outline of any other academic interactions that you have had with them (e.g., independent studies, supervised practical experiences, research, psychology club or department sponsored activities). Professors remember a lot of students, but they do not remember everything about every student. Making it easier for them will benefit you in the long run. Do not be afraid to let your references know if there is anything in particular that you would like them to highlight—for example, your work as a research assistant or a particular research project you conducted in a class. Finally, do not forget to thank your references and keep them posted on your progress. Writing letters of recommendation takes a lot of time and effort on their part. They have an investment in your future, too!

PERFORM WELL ON YOUR INTERVIEW

Top candidates are typically invited to campus for an interview. One of the primary purposes of an interview is to more closely assess how well you fit with the program. Therefore, it is essential that you prepare for the interview by reviewing everything about the program including its training model and goals, areas of concentration, and interests of the faculty. Be clear about your own interests and goals as well because it will be important that you clearly articulate how they match those of the program and program faculty. Taking time before the interview to reflect on these things will help you feel more confident and relaxed in the actual interview. A second primary purpose of the interview is for the admissions committee to informally assess a variety of personal characteristics (e.g., interpersonal skills, communication skills, confidence and clarity of purpose, personality style). Interviewers are looking for characteristics that make you stand out from the other candidates. Thus, use the interview as your opportunity to emphasize your strengths and special qualifications.

To further prepare for the interview, spend time thinking about possible questions that you may be asked. Review the list of potential questions in Exhibit 9.3 and think about your possible responses. Find a friend to role-play the interview with you and ask them to give you feedback on how well you presented yourself. Often, the career development cen-

EXHIBIT 9.3

Potential Interview Questions

What are your long-range career goals? Where do you hope to be in 5 years? Ten years?

Why did you decide to pursue a graduate degree in psychology?

Why did you apply to this particular program? Where did you hear about us?

Why should we accept you into our program?

How would you describe yourself?

What are the most important rewards you expect in your graduate training? In your career?

What are your greatest strengths and weaknesses?

How do you work under pressure? How do you handle stress?

Note. From American Psychological Association (2007c, p. 153).

ter at your college or university will provide mock interviews to assist you in this process. Also think about questions that you can ask of faculty. It is extremely important for you to ask questions during your interview because this demonstrates that you are interested in the program and in learning about available opportunities.

Interview formats vary. Some are a series of individual one-on-one interviews with faculty; others are group faculty interviews (i.e., you meet with two or three faculty members at a time) or group faculty–group student interviews (i.e., several applicants meet with several faculty members simultaneously). If you will be participating in the last type of interview, be sure to be active and assertive without dominating. Your goal is to be noticed and have your strengths noted while at the same time demonstrating socially and interpersonally appropriate behavior.

Important Considerations About Diversity in Your Choice of a Graduate Program

You may be interested in research or practice with a specific population such as women; members of racial or ethnic minority groups; gay, lesbian, or bisexual persons; or persons with disabilities. If you are a member of any of these groups or are interested in working with a particular population, you might begin to ask yourself how important it is for you to be in an environment with others like yourself or to work with faculty who are engaged in research or practice with these populations (APA, 2007c).

Members of underrepresented groups in psychology, such as racial or ethnic minorities, may wish to have someone of the same ethnicity as their mentor. Others might decide they would like a certain percentage of graduate students to be members of minority groups, not just for the support that they provide but also for the opportunity to work with, and learn from, others who are different from them. If so, you may want to pay particular attention to the percentage of faculty and students from various underrepresented groups. An alternative is to look for faculty members with good track records in working with different populations of students (APA, 2007c).

Lott (2005) identified three strategies for recruiting and retaining students of color. You may want to consider the degree to which each program you are considering attends to these strategies. They include (a) the use of admissions criteria that are flexible and sensitive to life experiences; (b) the use of a variety of creative recruitment strategies, including having faculty and ethnic minority students visit historically Black colleges and involving currently enrolled minority students in recruitment; and (c) financial assistance. Suggestions for retention and achievement include (a) ensuring the presence of a good percentage of minority faculty of color; (b) providing positive interactions with faculty; (c) providing mentors, networking, and encouragement to participate in teaching and research; and (d) providing an ethnically inclusive curriculum.

Minority students may want to know the answers to the following questions (see APA, 2007c, pp. 115–116).

1. How many minority students have been admitted to the program recently? How many finished their degrees? How does the retention rate for minorities compare with that for nonminorities?
2. What percentage of full-time faculty are members of ethnic minorities? What percentage of those faculty are tenured?
3. What kind of recruitment and retention strategies does the program use, in general and with regard to minority students in particular?
4. What kinds of organizations are available for community and support of students in general, and minority students in particular?
5. Are minority issues addressed in the curriculum? Is this done through a particular course, or integrated throughout the curriculum?

6. Is research about minorities valued and encouraged? Is there access to members of minority populations for such research? Is service to minorities possible during practicum?

How Do I Narrow My Options and Decide Which Program Is Right for Me?

If you are beginning to feel like you are on information overload, you are probably not alone. Remember that the best decisions are informed decisions. I will help you organize the information in a way that might help you to begin to narrow your options and offer a timeline to manage your tasks.

Make Some Tentative Choices

After reviewing your qualifications and reflecting on the opportunities in graduate programs of psychology, it is time to make some tentative choices. First, you should identify (a) the subfield of psychology that is the best match to your interests and skills, (b) the degree (i.e., PhD, PsyD, EdD) that best fits your needs, (c) your specific research and training interests, (d) theoretical orientation and training model preferences, and (e) any other prominent factors that would affect your choice of graduate programs (such as geographical location, costs, and demographic composition of students and faculty). Second, review graduate program offerings in the most recent edition of *Graduate Study in Psychology* with the aim of identifying all programs that meet your initial criteria and interests. That is, which programs best match your interests and needs? At this point, you may still be left with a list of programs that needs to be narrowed down. Give careful consideration to admissions criteria to find programs with criteria that best match your academic credentials (i.e., GPA, GRE scores, research experience, etc.). Begin to sort the programs into categories on the basis of the degree of fit between how well your credentials match the admissions criteria from each program. Try using the following categories as outlined in *Getting In: A Step-by-Step Plan for Gaining Admission to Graduate School in Psychology* (APA, 2007c, p. 108):

1. Strong bets: Your credentials exceed the required/preferred or median criteria (whichever is higher).

2. Good bets: Your credentials exceed the lower of the two ratings (i.e., required/preferred vs. the median), but do not exceed the higher. You also have strengths on nonobjective criteria programs highly value.
3. Long shots: Your credentials on one of the objective criteria fall slightly short of the required/preferred or median rating (whichever is lower).
4. Improbables: Your credentials on two or more of the objective criteria fall slightly short of the required/preferred or median rating (whichever is lower), or your rating on one of the objective criteria falls significantly below the required/preferred or median rating (whichever is lower).

At this point, you should eliminate the improbables and narrow the possibilities in the other categories to a manageable number. For the remaining programs, do some more exploration and research to gain additional information about the programs, faculty, and institutions within which they are housed. Begin with program Web sites, but do not be afraid to contact the programs and faculty directly or to visit the university. This is a good way to make yourself known to the program. After obtaining needed additional information, continue the comparison, ranking, and elimination process until you are left with approximately 10 schools to apply to. Remember, it is best to send the majority of your applications to programs that are good bets and to divide the rest between strong bets and long shots.

What if I Don't Get In?

It can be a disappointing experience not to be accepted into a graduate program. The first thing that you may want to do is to get an honest appraisal of your credentials from faculty whom you respect and trust (Landrum & Davis, 2007). They could be current faculty members in your undergraduate program, or faculty members of graduate programs to which you had hoped to gain admission. If the faculty you consult with identify some weaknesses, see what you can do to correct them. You might be able to retake courses, take additional courses, retake the GRE, or gain additional research or practical experience. Remember, determination and commitment are important qualities, not only to succeed once you are in graduate school but also as driving forces in gaining admission to a graduate program.

You also might want to reassess your goals and strategies. Spend some time reflecting on whether you selected programs carefully—paying attention to fit, the number of applications you submitted, the amount of time and effort you put into your letters of intent, and your choice of references (Kuther, 2006). Hard work and persistence often pay off!

Suggested Web Sites

- Psychology and Education Career Guidebook Series for Students of Color. This Web site provides guidebooks for high school and college students of color. It also provides guidebooks for college students of color applying to graduate school and professional programs: http://www.apa.org/pi/oema/careers/
- Psychology Graduate School Information: http://www.psychgrad.org/
- Union College: Careers and Graduate Study in Psychology: http://www.union.edu/PUBLIC/PSYDEPT/careers.htm
- Union College: Graduate School Information: http://www.union.edu/Career/Students/Seniors/GradSchool/index.php
- University of Washington: Career Center Information for Graduate Students: http://depts.washington.edu/careers/graduate/
- PsycCareers: APA's Online Career Center. In addition to information about the field of psychology, this Web site provides information for job seekers, including interview and resume tips: http://www.psyccareers.com/
- Nontraditional Careers in Psychology: http://www.apa.org/science/nonacad_careers.html
- Graduate Record Exam (GRE) Homepage: http://www.gre.org
- Miller Analogies Test: http://www.milleranalogies.com
- Information for Students From the APA Education Directorate: http://www.apa.org/ed/student.html
- American Psychological Association: Office of Accreditation: http://www.apa.org/ed/accreditation
- Association of State and Provincial Psychology Boards (ASPPB). ASPPB maintains a Web site with links to state psychology boards for information about licensure in each particular state: http://www.asppb.org

Suggested Reading

American Psychological Association. (2003). *Psychology: Scientific problem solvers: Careers for the twenty-first century.* Retrieved June 26, 2006, from http://www.apa.org/students/brochure/brochurenew.pdf

American Psychological Association. (2007). *Getting in: A step-by-step plan for gaining admission to graduate school in psychology* (2nd ed.). Washington, DC: Author.

American Psychological Association. (2007). *Graduate study in psychology.* Washington, DC: Author.

Bailey, D. S. (2004, April). Why accreditation matters. *gradPsych, 2*(2). Available online at http://gradpsych.apags.org/apr04/accreditation.cfm

Gleitman, H., Fridlund, A. J., & Reisberg, D. (2003). *Psychology* (6th ed.). New York: Norton.

Keith-Spiegel, P., & Wiederman, M. W. (2000). *The complete guide to graduate school admission: Psychology, counseling and related fields* (2nd ed.). Hillsdale, NJ: Erlbaum.

Kuther, T. L. (2004). *Getting into graduate school in psychology and related fields: Your guide to success.* Springfield, IL: Charles C Thomas.

Mayne, T. J., Norcross, J. G., & Sayette, M. A. (2004). *Insider's guide to graduate programs in clinical and counseling psychology.* New York: Guilford Press.

Norcross, J. C., Kohout, J. L., & Wicherski, M. (2006). Graduate admissions in psychology: II. Acceptance rates and financial considerations. *Eye on Psi Chi, 10*(3), 20–21, 32–33.

Sternberg, R. J. (2000). *Psychology: In search of the human mind* (3rd ed.). Fort Worth, TX: Harcourt College.

Sternberg, R. J. (Ed.). (2007). *Career paths in psychology: Where your degree can take you* (2nd ed.). Washington, DC: American Psychological Association.

Epilogue

A s you have seen from the chapters in this book, psychology is a broad and dynamic field. It intersects with disciplines that are both similar (e.g., counseling, social work) and bold and unique (e.g., cognitive neuroscience). Progress in the sciences and technology continues to push forward the bounds of knowledge, research, and practice in psychology. Globalization has advanced the field to the international level. Never before have issues of diversity and cross-cultural psychology offered as much creative tension between the opportunities and challenges associated with all aspects of studying and intervening in human behavior. As more people from diverse backgrounds enter the field, the magnitude of innovative practices in this science will grow exponentially.

Whether you are a young student just contemplating college or a person with experience considering a career change, the chapters in this book provide the basic resources to begin a productive process of exploration of yourself and your available educational and work options. This book will not provide the final answer to whether you should major in psychology. Instead, I hope this book has provided the tools and the knowledge that you need to make the right decision for you. From here, it takes motivation, support, hard work, and persistence. Having a road map and a compass is a start. Having a supportive person to make the journey with you is a help. Having the strength and confidence to believe in yourself and in your ability to cope effectively with the barriers and challenges that lie ahead is a must.

As you have no doubt learned from reading this book, career planning and decision making are part of a journey of self-awareness and discovery, not one-time events. Thus, the skills you have learned and the exercises you have engaged in here will serve as lifelong tools through school and into your career. For some people, this book might have been inspirational, for others it might have confirmed a hunch that psychology was a good match for them, for yet another group this book might have sent them off hunting for other educational and career alternatives. In every case, this book accomplished what I hoped it would. It is also my hope that this book has awakened a sense of curiosity in you that you may never have known you had, and that you now have the tools to explore your dreams and make them happen.

References

American Psychological Association. (2002). Ethical principles of psychologists and code of conduct. *American Psychologist, 57,* 1060–1073. Retrieved September 1, 2006, from http://www.apa.org/ethics/homepage.html

American Psychological Association. (2003). *Toward an inclusive psychology: Infusing the introductory psychology textbook with diversity content.* Retrieved March 14, 2006, from http://www.apa.org/pi/oema/inclusivepsychology.pdf

American Psychological Association. (2007a). *Accreditation.* Retrieved November 2, 2007, from http://www.apa.org/ed/accreditation/

American Psychological Association. (2007b). *Careers in psychology: Non-academic careers for scientific psychologists.* Retrieved November 1, 2007, from http://www.apa.org/science/nonacad_careers.html

American Psychological Association. (2007c). *Getting in: A step-by-step plan for gaining admission to graduate school in psychology* (2nd ed.). Washington, DC: Author.

American Psychological Association. (2007d). *Graduate education.* Retrieved November 2, 2007, from http://www.apa.org/ed/graduate/faqs.html

American Psychological Association. (2007e, June). *Table 3: Primary and secondary employment settings for 2005 psychology doctorate recipients by employment pattern*. Retrieved November 1, 2007, from http://research.apa.org/des05_t3.pdf

American Psychological Association Center for Psychology Workforce Analysis and Research. (2007). *2007 graduate study in psychology*. Unpublished analysis.

American Psychological Association Task Force on Distance Education and Training in Professional Psychology. (2002). *Principles of good practice in distance education and their application to professional education and training in psychology*. Retrieved January 2, 2006, from http://www.apa.org/ed/distance_ed.html

Amundson, N. E., Harris-Bowlsbey, J., & Niles, S. G. (2005). *Essential elements of career counseling: Processes and techniques*. Upper Saddle River, NJ: Pearson.

Appleby, D. (1999). Choosing a mentor. *Eye on Psi Chi, 3*(3), 38–39.

Appleby, D. (2000). Job skills valued by employers who interview psychology majors. *Eye on Psi Chi, 4*(3), 17.

Bandura, A. (1986). *Social foundations of thought and action: A social cognitive theory*. Englewood Cliffs, NJ: Prentice Hall.

Bandura, A. (1997). *Self-efficacy: The exercise of control*. New York: Freeman.

Benson, E. S. (2004). Behavioral genetics: Meet molecular biology. *Monitor on Psychology, 35*(4), 42–45.

Blocher, D. H., Heppner, M., & Johnston, J. (2001). *Career planning for the 21st century* (2nd ed.). Denver, CO: Love.

Blustein, D. L. (2006). *The psychology of working: A new perspective for career development, counseling, and public policy*. Mahwah, NJ: Erlbaum.

Blustein, D. L., Ellis, M. V., & Devenis, L. E. (1987). *Commitment to Career Choices Scale*. Unpublished manuscript.

Blustein, D. L., Ellis, M. V., & Devenis, L. E. (1989). The development and validation of a two dimensional model of the commitment to career choices process. *Journal of Vocational Behavior, 35*, 342–378.

Blustein, D. L., Schultheiss, D. E. P., & Flum, H. (2004). Toward a relational perspective of the psychology of careers and working: A social constructionist analysis. *Journal of Vocational Behavior, 64*, 423–440.

Bright, J. E. H., & Pryor, G. L. (2005). The chaos theory of careers: A user's guide. *Career Development Quarterly, 53*, 291–305.

Brown, D. (2002). The role of work values and cultural values in occupational choice, satisfaction, and success: A theoretical statement. In D. Brown & Associates (Eds.), *Career choice and development* (4th ed., pp. 465–509). San Francisco, CA: Jossey-Bass.

Burns, J. B. (2006). *Career opportunities in the nonprofit sector.* New York: Ferguson.

Bushe, G. R., & Kassam, A. F. (2005). When is appreciative inquiry transformational? A meta-case analysis. *Journal of Applied Behavioral Science, 41*(2), 161–181.

Buskist, W. (2001). Seven tips for preparing a successful application to graduate school in psychology. *Eye on Psi Chi, 5*(3), 32–34.

Campbell, D. (1974). *If you don't know where you're going, you'll probably end up somewhere else.* Allen, TX: Tabor.

Clay, R. A. (2005). On the practice horizon: Economic and demographic trends are among those changing the professional landscape. *Monitor on Psychology, 36*(2), 48–50, 52.

Cockley, K., Dreher, G. F., & Stockdale, M. S. (2004). Toward the inclusiveness and career success of African Americans in the workplace. In M. S. Stockdale & F. J. Crosby (Eds.), *Psychology and management of workplace diversity* (pp. 168–190). Malden, MA: Blackwell.

Collin, A., & Young, R. A. (1992). Constructing career through narrative and context: An interpretative perspective. In R. A. Young & A. Collin (Eds.), *Interpreting career: Hermeneutical studies of lives in context* (pp. 1–12). Westport, CT: Praeger.

Combs, P. (2000). *Major in success: Make college easier, fire up your dreams, and get a very cool job.* Berkeley, CA: Ten Speed Press.

Cone, J. D., & Foster, S. L. (1993). *Dissertations and theses from start to finish: Psychology and related fields.* Washington, DC: American Psychological Association.

Crosby, F. J., & Clayton, S. (2001). Affirmative action: Psychological contributions to policy. *Analyses of Social Issues and Public Policy, 1,* 71–87.

Dingfelder, S. F. (2004). To tell the truth. *Monitor on Psychology, 35*(3), 22–24.

Dingfelder, S. F. (2006a). Psychologists volunteer to help businesses rebuild. *Monitor on Psychology, 37*(9), 50.

Dingfelder, S. F. (2006b). Teaching self-care to Katrina's healers. *Monitor on Psychology, 37*(9), 43.

Dovidio, J. F., Gaertner, S. L., Kawakami, K., & Hodson, G. (2002). Why can't we just get along? Interpersonal biases and interracial distrust. *Cultural Diversity and Ethnic Minority Psychology, 8,* 88–102.

Ellis, A., & Dryden, W. (1997). *The practice of rational-emotive behavior therapy* (2nd ed.). New York: Springer Publishing Company.

Fuqua, D. R., Seaworth, T. B., & Newman, J. L. (1987). The relationship of career indecision and anxiety: A multivariate examination. *Journal of Vocational Behavior, 30,* 175–186.

Gati, I. (1996). Computer-assisted career counseling: Challenges and prospects. In M. L. Savickas & B. W. Walsh (Eds.), *Handbook of career counseling theory and practice* (pp. 169–190). Palo Alto, CA: Davies-Black.

Gati, I., & Asher, I. (2001). Prescreening, in-depth exploration, and choice: From decision theory to career counseling practice. *Career Development Quarterly, 50,* 140–157.

Gati, I., Krausz, M., & Osipow, S. H. (1996). A taxonomy of difficulties in career decision making. *Journal of Counseling Psychology, 43,* 510–526.

Gelatt, H. B. (1989). Positive uncertainty: A new decision-making framework for counseling. *Journal of Counseling Psychology, 33,* 252–256.

Gelatt, H. B. (1991). *Creative decision-making: Using positive uncertainty.* Los Altos, CA: Crisp.

Germer, C. K. (2005). Anxiety disorders: Befriending fear. In C. K. Germer, R. D. Siegel, & P. R. Fulton (Eds.), *Mindfulness and psychotherapy* (pp. 152–172). New York: Guilford Press.

Germer, C. K., Siegel, R. D., & Fulton, P. R. (Eds.). (2005). *Mindfulness and psychotherapy.* New York: Guilford Press.

Gleitman, H., Fridlund, A. J., & Reisberg, D. (2003). *Basic psychology* (5th ed.). New York: Norton.

Gmelch, G. (1997). Crossing cultures: Student travel and personal development. *International Journal of Intercultural Relations, 21,* 475–490.

Gottfredson, G. D., & Holland, J. L. (1996). *Dictionary of Holland occupational codes* (3rd ed.). Odessa, FL: Psychological Assessment Resources.

Gurin, P., Nagda, B. A., & Lopez, G. E. (2004). The benefits of diversity in education for democratic citizenship. *Journal of Social Issues, 60,* 17–34.

Hammer, A. L. (1993). *Introduction to type and careers.* Mountain View, CA: CPP.

Hogan, J. D., & Gielen, U. P. (2004). International psychology: Past, present and future. *Eye on Psi Chi, 8*(2), 14–15.

Holland, J. L. (1994). *Self-directed search*. Odessa, FL: Psychological Assessment Resources.

Holland, J. L. (1997). *Making vocational choices: A theory of vocational personalities and work environments* (3rd ed.). Odessa, FL: Psychological Assessment Resources.

Holland, J. L. (2000). *The occupations finder*. Odessa, FL: Psychological Assessment Resources.

Huff, C. (2004). The baggage screener's brain scan. *Monitor on Psychology, 35*(8), 34–36.

Jones, J. M. (1996). *Prejudice and racism* (2nd ed.). New York: McGraw-Hill.

Kaplan, D. M., & Brown, D. (1987). The role of anxiety in career indecisiveness. *Career Development Quarterly, 36,* 148–162.

Keith-Spiegel, P., Tabachnick, B. G., & Spiegel, G. B. (1994). When demand exceeds supply: Second-order criteria used by graduate school selection committees. *Teaching of Psychology, 21,* 79–81.

Keith-Spiegel, P., & Wiederman, M. W. (2000). *The complete guide to graduate school admission: Psychology, counseling and related fields* (2nd ed.). Hillsdale, NJ: Erlbaum.

Kersting, K. (2005). Health-care calling: Psychologists' roles in health care are well established and growing. *Monitor on Psychology, 36(2),* 56–58.

Kluger, A. N., & Nir, D. (2006, July). *Feedforward first, feedback later*. Paper presented at the 26th International Congress of Applied Psychology. Athens, Greece.

Koch, C. (2002). Getting involved by getting a mentor. *Eye on Psi Chi, 6*(3), 28.

Kohout, J., & Wicherski, M. (2007). *2005 doctorate employment survey*. Washington, DC: American Psychological Association.

Krannich, R. I. (1991). *Careering and re-careering for the 1990's: The complete guide to planning your future*. Woodbridge, VA: Impact.

Kuther, T. L. (2006). *The psychology major's handbook* (2nd ed.). Belmont, CA: Thomson.

Kuther, T. L., & Morgan, R. D. (2004). *Careers in psychology: Opportunities in a changing world*. Belmont, CA: Wadsworth.

Landrum, R. E., & Davis, S. F. (2004). *The psychology major: Career options and strategies for success* (2nd ed.). Upper Saddle River, NJ: Pearson Education.

Landrum, R. E., & Davis, S. F. (2007). *The psychology major: Career options and strategies for success* (3rd ed.). Upper Saddle River, NJ: Pearson Education.

Law School Admission Council. (2006). *Think about law school.* Retrieved November 1, 2007, from http://www.lsac.org/pdfs/2006-2007/ThinkAboutLawSchool2006.pdf

Lenox, R. A., & Subich, L. M. (1994a). The relationship between self-efficacy beliefs and inventoried vocational interests. *Career Development Quarterly, 42,* 302–313.

Lenox, R. A., & Subich, L. M. (1994b). *Self-Efficacy Questionnaire.* Unpublished manuscript.

Lent, R. W., Brown, S. D., & Hackett, G. (1994). Toward a unified social cognitive theory of career and academic interest, choice, and performance. *Journal of Vocational Behavior, 45,* 79–122.

LoCicero, A., & Hancock, J. (2000). Preparing students for success in fieldwork. *Teaching of Psychology, 27,* 117–120.

Lott, B. (2005). *Strategies for recruitment, retention, and achievement of minority students of color in psychology graduate programs.* Unpublished manuscript.

Lunneborg, P. W., & Wilson, V. M. (1987). Three keys to graduate psychology. In P. J. Woods & C. S. Wilkinson (Eds.), *Is psychology the major for you? Planning your undergraduate years* (pp. 89–104). Washington, DC: American Psychological Association.

Martin, J. N., & Rohrlich, B. (1991). The relationship between study abroad, student expectations and selected student characteristics. *Journal of College Student Development, 32,* 39–49.

Maton, K. I., Kohout, J. L., Wicherski, M., Leary, G. E., & Vinokurov, A. (2006). Minority students of color and the psychology graduate pipeline: Disquieting and encouraging trends, 1989–2003. *American Psychologist, 61,* 117–131.

McCaslin, S. (2003). How can I do it? The aspiring international psychologist: A student perspective. *Eye on Psi Chi, 7*(2), 24–26.

McGovern, T. V., Furumoto, L., Halpern, D. F., Kimble, G. A., & McKeachie, W. J. (1991). Liberal education, study in depth, and the arts and sciences major—Psychology. *American Psychologist, 46,* 598–605.

Myers, I. B. (1993). *Gifts differing.* Palo Alto, CA: Consulting Psychologists Press.

Myers, I. B. (1998). *Introduction to type* (6th ed.). Mountain View, CA: CPP.

Myers, I. B., McCaulley, M. H., Quenk, N. L., & Hammer, A. L. (1998). *MBTI manual: A guide to the development and use of the Myers–Briggs Type Indicator* (3rd ed.). Palo Alto, CA: Consulting Psychologists Press.

National Center on Educational Statistics. (n.d.). *Digest of educational statistics 2005: Table 249. Bachelor's degrees conferred by degree-granting institutions, by discipline division: Selected years, 1970–71 through 2003–04.* Retrieved October 26, 2007, from http://nces.ed.gov/programs/digest/d05/tables/dt05_249.asp

Nauta, M. M. (2002). A career research project for undergraduate psychology students. *Teaching of Psychology, 29,* 288–291.

Norcross, J. C., Kohout, J. L., & Wicherski, M. (2006). Graduate admissions in psychology: I. The application process. *Eye on Psi Chi, 10*(2), 28–29.

North Carolina State Occupational Information Coordinating Committee. (n.d.). *Holland Personality Types & Work Environments, Occupations and College Majors.* Retrieved October 30, 2007, from http://www.soicc.state.nc.us/soicc/planning/jh-types.htm

Okun, B. F., Fried, J., & Okun, M. L. (1999). *Understanding diversity: A learning-as-practice primer.* Pacific Grove, CA: Brooks/Cole.

Psi Chi, the National Honor Society in Psychology. (2002–2007). *Becoming a member.* Retrieved November 1, 2007, from http://www.psichi.org/about/becomember.asp

Rogers, M. R., & Molina, L. E. (2006). Exemplary efforts in psychology to recruit and retain graduate students of color. *American Psychologist, 61,* 143–156.

Rosen, D., Holmberg, K., & Holland, J. L. (1994). *The Educational Opportunities Finder.* Odessa, FL: Psychological Assessment Resources.

Saka, N., Gati, I., & Kelly, K. R. (2006). *Emotional and personality-related aspects of career decision-making difficulties.* Unpublished manuscript, Department of Psychology, Hebrew University of Jerusalem, Israel.

Sarason, I. G., & Sarason, B. R. (2002). *Abnormal psychology: The problem of maladaptive behavior* (10th ed.). Upper Saddle River, NJ: Prentice Hall.

Schultheiss, D. E. P. (2003). A relational approach to career counseling: Theoretical integration and practical application. *Journal of Counseling and Development, 81,* 301–310.

Schultheiss, D. E. P., Palma, T. V., Predragovich, K. S., & Glasscock, J. M. J. (2002). Relational influences on career paths: Siblings in context. *Journal of Counseling Psychology, 49,* 302–310.

Schultheiss, D. E. P., & Stead, G. B. (2004). Construct validity of the Career Myths Scale among South African adolescents. *Journal of Psychology in Africa, 14,* 9–15.

Sharf, R. S. (2006). *Applying career development theory to counseling* (4th ed.). Belmont, CA: Thomson Wadsworth.

Singleton, D., Tate, A. C., & Kohout, J. L. (2003). *2002 Master's, Specialist's, and Related Degrees Employment Survey.* Retrieved June 21, 2006, from http://research.apa.org/2002mes.pdf

Stead, G. B. (1991). *The Career Myths Scale.* Unpublished manuscript, Vista University, Port Elizabeth, South Africa.

Stead, G. B., & Watson, M. B. (1993). The Career Myths Scale: Its validity and applicability. *International Journal for the Advancement of Counselling, 16,* 89–97.

Stead, G. B., & Watson M. B. (2006). Career decision making and career indecision. In G. B. Stead & M. B. Watson (Eds.), *Career psychology in the South African context* (2nd ed., pp. 94–109). Hatfield, Pretoria, South Africa: Van Schaik.

Sternberg, R. J. (2000). *Psychology: In search of the human mind* (3rd ed.). Fort Worth, TX: Harcourt College.

Sternberg, R. J. (2005). Producing tomorrow's leaders—In psychology and everything else. *Eye on Psi Chi, 10*(1), 14–15.

Stoloff, M., Sanders, N., & McCarthy, M. (2005). *Profiles of undergraduate programs in psychology.* Retrieved November 19, 2005, from http://www.apa.org/ed/pcue/profiles_intro.html

Sue, D. W., & Sue, D. (1990). *Counseling the culturally different: Theory and practice.* New York: Wiley.

A taxonomy of career decision-making difficulties. (2001–2006). Retrieved August 17, 2006, from http://kivunim.huji.ac.il/cddq/theory.htm

Trimble, J. E., Stevenson, M. R., Worell, J. P., & the APA Commission on Ethnic Minority Recruitment, Retention, and Training Task Force Textbook Initiative Work Group. (2003). *Toward an inclusive psychology: Infusing the introductory psychology textbook with diversity content.* Washington, DC: American Psychological Association.

University of Missouri—Columbia. (2007). *The Career Interests Game.* Retrieved October 31, 2007, from http://career.missouri.edu/students/explore/thecareerinterestsgame.php

U.S. Bureau of Labor Statistics. (n.d.). *Occupational outlook handbook (OOH), 2006–07 edition.* Retrieved October 24, 2006, from http://www.bls.gov/oco/

U.S. Census Bureau. (2002). *Statistical abstract of the United States: 2002 (Table 15. Resident population by Hispanic origin status, p. 17).* Retrieved November 15, 2007, from http://www.census.gov/prod/2003pubs/02statab/pop.pdf

U.S. News & World Report. (2007). *America's best graduate schools 2008.* Retrieved November 2, 2007, from http://grad-schools.usnews.rankingsandreviews.com/usnews/edu/grad/rankings/about/index_brief.php

Vasquez, M. J. T., & Jones, J. M. (2006). Increasing the number of psychologists of color: Public policy issues for affirmative diversity. *American Psychologist, 61,* 132–142

Vasquez, M. J. T., Lott, B., Garcia-Vazquez, E., Grant, S. K., Iwamasa, G. Y., Molina, L. E., et al. (2006). Personal reflections: Barriers and strategies in increasing diversity in psychology. *American Psychologist, 61,* 157–172.

Vasquez, M. J. T., & Reyes, C. J. (2004). If only I knew then what I know now: Perspectives of a woman of color. *Eye on Psi Chi, 8*(3), 18–19, 33–35.

Vignoli, E., Croity-Belz, S., Chapeland, V., de Fillipis, A., & Garcia, M. (2005). Career exploration in adolescents: The role of anxiety, attachment, and parenting style. *Journal of Vocational Behavior, 67,* 153–168.

Wallace, B. A., & Shapiro, S. L. (2006). Mental balance and well-being: Building bridges between Buddhism and Western Psychology. *American Psychologist, 61,* 690–701.

Wiley, J. D. (2001). Foreword. In R. A. Ibarra (Ed.), *Beyond affirmative action: Reframing the context of higher education* (pp. xi–xii). Madison: University of Wisconsin Press.

Winerman, L. (2005a). The mind's mirror. *Monitor on Psychology, 36*(9), 49–50.

Winerman, L. (2005b). A virtual cure. *Monitor on Psychology, 36*(7), 87–89.

Xu, W., & Leffler, A. (1996). Gender and race effects on occupational prestige, segregation, and earnings. In E. N. Chow & D. Y. Wilkinson (Eds.), *Race, class, & gender: Common bonds, different voices* (pp. 107–124). Thousand Oaks, CA: Sage.

Index

About the Author

Donna E. Palladino Schultheiss, PhD, is a professor in the Department of Counseling, Administration, Supervision, and Adult Learning at Cleveland State University, Cleveland, Ohio. She earned her doctoral degree in counseling psychology from the University at Albany, State University of New York. She is currently codirector of training for the counseling psychology specialization in the urban education doctoral program at Cleveland State, where she teaches in both the doctoral and master's programs. She serves as chair elect of the Society for Vocational Psychology, a section of the American Psychological Association Division 17 (Society of Counseling Psychology), and is past chair of the Research Committee for the National Career Development Association. She also currently serves as the U.S. national liaison for the International Association of Applied Psychologists Division 15 (Counseling Psychology). In 2006, she received an award for the most outstanding research contribution to *Career Development Quarterly.* Dr. Schultheiss has written several book chapters and numerous articles in a number of journals, including *Journal of Counseling Psychology, The Counseling Psychologist, Professional Psychology: Research and Practice, Journal of Vocational Behavior, Career Development Quarterly, Journal of Career Development,* and *Journal of Career Assessment.* She also has published in several international journals, including *International Journal of Educational and Vocational Guidance, L'Orientation Scolaire et Professionnelle, Giornale Italiano di Psicologia dell'Orientamento, South African Journal of Psychology,* and *Journal of Psychology in Africa.* She serves on the editorial boards of *Journal of Counseling Psychology* and *Journal of Vocational Behavior.*